38   García Márquez: El coronel no tiene
quien le escriba

Critical Guides to Spanish Texts

EDITED BY J.E. VAREY AND A.D. DEYERMOND

GARCÍA MÁRQUEZ

El coronel no tiene quien le escriba

Ben Box

Editor, *The South American Handbook*

Grant & Cutler Ltd *in association with*
Tamesis Books Ltd **1990**

ISBN 0 7293 0174 5

I.S.B.N. 84-499-7183-7
DEPÓSITO LEGAL: V. 1.699 - 1990

Printed in Spain by
Artes Gráficas Soler, S.A., Valencia
for
GRANT AND CUTLER LTD
55-57 GREAT MARLBOROUGH STREET, LONDON, W1V 2AY

Contents

Preface

References to the text of *El coronel no tiene quien le escriba* are to the edition of Giovanni Pontiero (*1*). This is the only edition easily available which contains an introduction, notes and vocabulary. Other editions are given in the Bibliographical Note (see under *1*).

The figures in parentheses in italic type refer to the numbered items in the Bibliographical Note; where necessary these are followed by page numbers, thus: (*10*, p.70). The main body of criticism on the works of García Márquez has concentratred on *Cien años de soledad*, and more recently, on *El otoño del patriarca*, so that attention to *El coronel no tiene quien le escriba* has often been limited to brief introductory remarks or résumés. The Bibliographical Note includes some of this type of study, which may be of background interest to the student, as well as those articles and books specifically dealing with *El coronel*. References to some other studies will be found in footnotes.

Certain parts of chapter 5 were presented at a lecture at Clifton College, Bristol, on 19 November, 1982, and I am grateful to Mr John Gibbs for inviting me to air my ideas in public. I am also very grateful to Professor A.D. Deyermond and to Professor J.E. Varey who read the typescript and made many helpful comments, and to Sarah Cameron for reading the typescript, and for her continual encouragement.

1 *Introduction*

El coronel no tiene quien le escriba was written by Gabriel García Márquez in Paris in 1956 and 1957. At this time, García Márquez was unemployed and destitute since the Colombian newspaper, *El Espectador*, for which he worked had been closed down by General Rojas Pinilla, the Colombian dictator. As has often been remarked, García Márquez's desperate situation reminded him of a scene that he had encountered in Barranquilla, Northern Colombia: he saw on several occasions a man watching the boats, waiting anxiously outside the fish market. This in turn recalled his own grandfather who had been waiting for many years for the recognition of his services in the Liberal forces during The War of 1000 Days, fought between 1899 and 1902. These inspirational images were then transformed into the episode of an ageing colonel awaiting his pension; this originally formed part of a novel, first entitled *La casa*, later to become *La mala hora* (see *1*, pp.viii-ix; *16*, p.39; *28*, p.35; *33*, pp.46-48). Having extracted the episode, García Márquez rewrote it nine times (*28*, p.88, also *23*, p.336; but Conte says three times, *12*, p.169, and Vargas Llosa says eleven, *33*, p.48).

El coronel was first published in 1958, but its merits were not fully recognised until the success of *Cien años de soledad* had brought García Márquez world-wide acclaim. Many critics have referred to the novel as a masterpiece, or an example of perfection (for instance, *1*, p.vii; *12*, p.165; *26*, p.114; *30*, p.19). The brevity of the novel masks a skilful control of narrative technique and an ability to present human dilemmas, particularly as witnessed in a mid-twentieth-century Colombian context, with masterly concision.

The story describes three months in the life of an anonymous Colonel who lives in a remote town in the tropical zone of Northern Colombia. He is a veteran of a civil war that took place at the turn of the twentieth century and he has been waiting since then for a pension from the Government, guaranteed at the end of hostilities. He and his wife are poverty-stricken and starving, and their house is mortgaged.

The period is October to December in the year of the Suez Crisis (1956); fighting is taking place in the interior of the country, a state of siege exists in the town, there is a nightly curfew; because of censorship, clandestine information is passed amongst the inhabitants (including the Colonel). For this latter activity, the Colonel's son Agustín was killed by the police in the cockpit, the arena in which fighting cocks were matched. Agustín, a hard-working tailor, left his parents a sewing-machine (which they sold—their last source of income) and a fighting cock. Whether the cock should be sold is a major bone of contention between the Colonel and his wife: feeding it deprives them of much of their already scant resources, but the Colonel regards it as his duty to his son to set the cock in the pit in the forthcoming cockfights in January. During their anxious waiting for a letter, and their deliberations over the cock, they meet various members of the town's society: the revolutionary doctor; the priest who censors the films; their black lawyer whom they decide to change in the hope of speeding up the receipt of a pension; Moisés, a Syrian shop-keeper; the town's rich man, Don Sabas, who might buy the cock; and Agustín's former colleagues who undertake to feed the cock until January.

During the three months in which these events take place, the Colonel's anxieties are interlaced with his memories of the past fifty-six years, and with his hopes for the future. As the weather changes from the hot, wet winter of October to spring in December, the Colonel ends his vacillations about selling the cock and resolves to keep it. Nevertheless, this provides no solution to the problem of how to feed his wife and himself. The cock may not win its fight, which would deprive them of winnings and a good sale price, and still no letter from the Government has come on the weekly mail launch.

The few events of *El coronel* take place in a sketchily-drawn environment. The story is set in an unnamed town, referred to as 'el pueblo'. It is accessible only by river, and even then by a journey lasting eight hours: 'Los viajeros descendieron estragados después de ocho horas sin cambiar de posición' (13). We are not told where the journey begins. The mail launch arrives every Friday, and with the mail come the newspapers. The description of the town rests on only a few details:

> El coronel descendió hacia la plaza por un callejón de casas apelotonadas...Hasta donde alcanza su vista el pueblo estaba tapizado de flores. (7)

> Lo persiguió por la calle paralela al puerto, un laberinto de almacenes y barracas con mercancías de colores en exhibición. (13-14)

> Los almendros de la plaza soltaban sus últimas hojas podridas. (15)

> El betún de las calles empezaba a fundirse con el calor. (19)

Among the more frequently mentioned places are the quay, a tailor's shop, a cinema, a billiard hall, and the scene of the most lively activity, a cockpit. From the heat, rain, and constant references to mosquitoes, the town must be in the tropics.

Two other towns are mentioned in the text, both of which fix, and widen, the focus of the book on the tropical north of Colombia. One is Manaure (where the Colonel attended school, 33), which is on the Guajira Peninsula. The other is Macondo (from which the Colonel fled in the banana boom, 51). The latter is the fictional name for Aracataca, García Márquez's birthplace in the Department of Magdalena. It is the setting for *Cien años de soledad*, *La hojarasca* and 'La siesta del martes', 'Un día después del sábado', and 'Los funerales de la Mamá Grande' (in *Los funerales de la Mamá Grande*). 'El pueblo', besides being the Colonel's home town in *El coronel*, is also the setting for *La mala hora*, 'Un día de éstos', 'En este pueblo no hay ladrones', 'La prodigiosa tarde de Baltasar' and 'Rosas artificiales' (in *Los funerales de la Mamá Grande*). (See *28*, p.78; *33*, p.345, and *21*, p.18.)

For two major reasons, some critics imply that Macondo and

'el pueblo' can be combined in García Márquez's fiction before
Cien años de soledad. The first reason is a desire to show that
the Macondo/'el pueblo' setting is representative of Colombia
or Latin America as a whole (*10*, p.18; *17*, pp.324-25; *30*, p.19;
36, pp.81-84; *26*, pp.64-69). The second reason is based on the
belief that García Márquez was creating a fictitious world that
evolves from story to story so that each work is a fragment of a
vast whole, culminating in *Cien años de soledad*. Vargas Llosa,
although emphasising the differences between the two towns by
saying that 'el pueblo' is not the Macondo of García Márquez's
memory and imagination (*33*, p.167), echoes the implication
that they form a joint location because Macondo retroactively
absorbs 'el pueblo' (*33*, p.105).[1] A number of critics point out
the strong links between *Cien años de soledad* and the earlier
works (for instance, *9*, p.64; *8*, p.9; *21*, p.18) and it is true that
certain characters, scenes and images do appear in more than
one story. Some, like Colonel Aureliano Buendía, are not tied to
any particular setting; others link the two settings and therefore
different stories: the Colonel leaves Macondo for 'el pueblo' in
the banana boom, Padre Ángel is transferred from Macondo to
'el pueblo'. But in stories which have a common setting, the
links are much stronger: the plague of dead birds in 'Un día
después del sábado' and *Cien años de soledad*; the dentist
treating the mayor of 'el pueblo' in 'Un día de éstos' and *La
mala hora*; and a great many between *La mala hora* and *El
coronel* (the censorship of films, Moisés, the Syrian shopkeeper,
the river traffic, etc). In justification of this, García Márquez
himself has stated that all his early works lead up to *Cien años de
soledad*, and that 'En realidad, uno no se escribe sino un libro'
(*28*, p.77; *1*, p.xv).

The difference between the two settings of 'el pueblo' and
Macondo are readily apparent:

> Macondo es un lugar ardiente, cenagoso, fuera del tiempo,
> arruinado y lleno de historias fantásticas, cuya única
> comunicación con el mundo depende de un trencito

---

[1] He adds that the marine setting of 'El mar del tiempo perdido' (written by
García Márquez in 1961) is similarly absorbed (*33*, p.463).

amarillo, aunque no se sabe adónde conduce; "el pueblo" es más real, está infestado por los odios políticos y el chismorreo perverso, y tiene un apestoso río por donde llega una lancha con el correo dos veces por semana.[2]

Vargas Llosa notes that the principal physical difference between the two towns is that 'el pueblo' has a river, although the flora, fauna and tropical weather of the two are the same.

The model for 'el pueblo' is said by Vargas Llosa and Pontiero to be Sucre (which was one of the homes of García Márquez's parents: *33*, p.105; *1*, p.vii). This town is situated on the Caño Mojano in the tissue of lowland swamps between the rivers Magdalena and Cauca.[3] Taking 'el pueblo' to be Sucre, Vargas Llosa reveals a further distinguishing factor in that 'el pueblo'/Sucre is within the area of Colombia that was affected by the civil war known as *La Violencia*, but Macondo (or its model Aracataca), being closer to the Atlantic Coast, was not involved; moreover, Macondo is in the banana-growing zone, but 'el pueblo' is not.

The stories set in Macondo contain more subjective criteria and more interiorised, psychological material which tends towards a universal interpretation. 'El pueblo', on the other hand, is part of an objective, socio-political narrative and is described, along with its occupants and their lives, in a style pared down to a suitable directness (*33*, pp.299-300; see also *21*, pp.19-20). Of the style of *El coronel*, Gullón says:

> *El coronel no tiene quien le escriba*, admirable en la lúcida intensidad con que se integran personaje, situación y sociedad; admirable, quizá todavía más, por la tersura narrativa, no alcanza a crear, como *Cien años*, un vasto mundo imaginativo donde se cruzan espectros familiares con sombras de imprecisa realidad, un mundo variado y

[2] José Miguel Oviedo, 'Macondo, un territorio mágico y americano', in *Sobre García Márquez*, pp.44-53, at p.48. In fact, in *El coronel*, the mail launch arrives once a week, on Friday.

[3] In his review of *Crónica de una muerte anunciada*, Pepe Fajardo says that the setting of this novel is also Sucre: *Istoé* (São Paulo), 6 May 1981, 46-47.

riquísimo del cual el viejo coronel, en dilatada espera, pudiera ser habitante conspicuo. *(22*, p.144)

But it is not reasonable to compare the scope and intentions of *El coronel* with those of *Cien años de soledad*, just as it can be dangerous to seek common denominators between *El coronel* and García Márquez's other works. In so doing the work's individual qualities may be clouded and its right to be considered on its own denied.

As Vargas Llosa says, the directness of style of *El coronel* is adapted to suit the content of the story. Its concision is not evident in *Cien años de soledad* because the vast, imaginative world requires a more expansive style. García Márquez's attitude to the content of *El coronel* and *La mala hora* has tended to isolate these two novels:

> Entonces empecé a contar un tipo de historia que era totalmente distinto del que me interesaba antes, dramas [*El coronel, La mala hora*] relacionados directamente con el problema social y político de Colombia en esos momentos...
> Al decirte que me encontré con estos temas un poco ajenos a mí, ya te estoy confesando cosas que realmente son muy profundas para mí...(Carmen Arnau, *8*, p.14, quoting a conversation between García Márquez and Mario Vargas Llosa)

Arnau takes this to mean that 'tanto *El coronel no tiene quien le escriba* como *La mala hora*, son dos obras que no cree profundamente sinceras, rehusa darles como marco Macondo' (*8*, p.14). But is the phrase 'un poco ajenos' the same as 'no...profundamente sinceras'? Pontiero demonstrates admirably that at least in *El coronel* there is no lack of commitment on the author's part:

> For García Márquez there exists no real conflict between art and commitment so long as the writer draws inspiration from the reality he knows and understands. Every novel he

has written to date falls into this category. But a deep concern with humanitarian principles is never allowed to obscure his main objective as a writer intent upon perfection of technique. (*1*, p.xlii)

The apparent contradictions in García Márquez's statements about writing only one book, but wishing to put *El coronel, La mala hora* and *Los funerales de la Mamá Grande* in parentheses (to use Gilard's phrase, *20*, p.16) are more understandable if one recognises that the books are part of a process of experimentation with technique which lends each one an 'intriguing vitality'.[4] In the case of *El coronel* this vitality expresses García Márquez's political sensibilities of the time, and his preoccupation with an individual's struggle to retain his dignity and will to survive in the face of two things: a corrupt and unyielding environment, and the unrelenting passage of time towards death. The setting of the novel in 'el pueblo' acts as a signature for the political bias of the content and the unique precision of the style (see chapters 2 and 5 below) during the evolution of García Márquez's writing.

[4] Roger M. Peel, 'The Short Stories of Gabriel García Márquez', *Studies in Short Fiction*, 8 (1971), 159-68, at p.161.

2 *The Setting in Time*

Neither politics nor social problems provides the foreground of the novel: each provides an essential perspective against which the principal events may be viewed. References to the two civil wars mentioned in the story are vague; as Vargas Llosa describes them, they are 'un horizonte épico y multicolor, algo tan llamativo como distante y confuso' (*33*, p.117). However, there are hints and indications of these and other historical events, some of which would be clear enough to the native reader.

The story's timespan lasts from October to December, 1956, that is to say, the end of the hot, wet Caribbean winter, and the beginning of spring. The heat and the down-pours are often shown, usually linked with a character's health, or state of mind: ' "Ya no llueve más", pensó el coronel, y se sintió mejor' (10); 'El calor de la tarde estimuló el dinamismo de la mujer' (20). This becomes particularly noticeable when the weather improves in December: 'No necesitó abrir la ventana para identificar a diciembre. Lo descubrió en sus propios huesos cuando picaba en la cocina las frutas para el desayuno del gallo' (62). The symbolic significance of the weather will be dealt with below, in chapter 4.

We know that the year whose end we witness is 1956, not because of any reference to the date itself, but from a reference to the nationalisation of the Suez Canal, which happened in July, leading to the crisis in November of that year: 'Arriba, a cuatro columnas, una crónica sobre la nacionalización del canal de Suez' (15).[5] The reference to Suez occurs in a newspaper that the doctor gives to the Colonel after the latter has discovered on yet another Friday that there is no letter for him. The reference not only serves to fix the narrative in history, but also reveals

[5] García Márquez refers to the Suez Crisis in his article, 'El año más famoso del mundo', included in *Cuando era feliz e indocumentado* (Caracas: Ediciones el Ojo del Camello, 1973), pp.9-28.

that Colombian papers do not give domestic affairs headline treatment: 'El coronel leyó los titulares destacados. Noticias internacionales' (15). In itself this would not be important, but in 1956, Colombia was in the middle of *La Violencia*, when, among other repressive measures, press censorship was in force: 'Es difícil leer entre líneas lo que permite publicar la censura' (15). Previously in the narrative, this political situation had been hinted at: 'en estado de sitio' (10); 'por distribuir información clandestina' (12), and others follow, for example: 'la resistencia armada en el interior del país' (18); the curfew; moral censorship (48); the police raid on the billiard hall (61).

While the newspapers concentrate on international affairs, those inhabitants of the town who wish to know what is going on around them (the doctor, the Colonel, the tailor's apprentices) have either to read between the lines of the press, or receive clandestine information (for the distribution of which the Colonel's son was killed). The network of resistance that passes on this information is well-established, and the doctor and the apprentices give the Colonel notes to read (the doctor on p.18; the apprentices on p.39 and p.60). The Colonel's reaction, however, is both cynical and depressed: 'Se sintió demolido. Diez años de informaciones clandestinas no le habían ensenãdo que ninguna noticia era más sorprendente que la del mes entrante' (18).

On the other hand, those who do not wish to know about the state of affairs cannot escape the repression, seen in the state of siege, the curfew and the moral censorship of films by the priest. But there is no drama in this for them because it is an accepted way of life. Don Sabas says: 'Siempre me olvida que estamos en estado de sitio' (10); people still go to the cinema (48); the Colonel uses the curfew bell at eleven o'clock to set his watch (49). Just as the secret information depresses the Colonel, so does the numbing effect of the repression.

No se arrepintió. Desde hacía mucho tiempo el pueblo yacía en una especie de sopor, estragado por diez años de historia. Esa tarde—otro viernes sin carta—la gente había despertado. El coronel se acordó de otra época. Se vio a sí

mismo con su mujer y su hijo asistiendo bajo el paraguas a
un espectáculo que no fue interrumpido a pesar de la
lluvia...(66)

The tedious, corrupt present, and his own situation in it, causes
the Colonel to reminisce about both the rosy and the unpleasant
events of the past. In this way, two real, and a number of
fictional, historical events are insinuated into the story.

The first real occurrence, chronologically, is the civil war of
1899 to 1902, known as The War of 1000 Days. References to
this tragedy, in which 100,000 people died, concentrate in *El
coronel* on the Treaty of Neerlandia (29, 31, 51), the first peace
of the war. Fighting began in the impoverished coffee zones
following a drastic fall in coffee prices between 1896 and 1899.
The Liberal opposition rebelled on 20 October 1899 against a
Conservative Government that faced financial crisis and a split
in its party ranks. The Liberals, in commencing the war, had no
policy or definite objective (nor an army, nor finances for that
matter), and at its conclusion, each political faction had
disintegrated, paving the way for the dictatorship of Rafael
Reyes. Joaquín Tamayo says of the Liberals: 'Rara vez en la
historia un partido político se ha suicidado en tal forma, sin
hacer caso de múltiples circunstancias adversas, y sin querer
escuchar la voz sensata de sus directores' (*42*, p.38). The leaders
in question were Generals Figueredo and Rafael Uribe Uribe,
who called on the Liberals not to begin the Revolution in 1899.
The latter, whom Vargas Llosa shows to be a model for all
García Márquez's colonels, but particularly Coronel Aureliano
Buendía (*33*, p.123; see also *28*, p.21), signed the Treaty of
Neerlandia with the Conservative General Juan B. Tobar on 24
October 1902.[6] The war was concluded by a second treaty signed
on board the United States Warship *Wisconsin*, on 21 November
1902, by the Liberal leader in the Panamanian isthmus,
Benjamín Herrera; this treaty led to Panama's secession from
Colombia in 1903, giving the USA access for the construction of

---

[6] Bergquist (*38*, pp.186-87) and García Márquez in *El coronel* and *Cien años de
soledad* call it the Treaty of Neerlandia; Tamayo calls it Nerlandia. Pontiero says
that the Treaty is fictional, which clearly it is not (*1*, p.viii).

the Panama Canal.

Another episode of twentieth-century Colombian history that is touched upon in *El coronel* is that of the banana boom (dealt with in far greater depth in *La hojarasca* and *Cien años de soledad*). We are told:

> Se acordó de Macondo. El coronel esperó diez años a que se cumplieron las promesas de Neerlandia. En el sopor de la siesta vio llegar un tren amarillo y polvoriento con hombres y mujeres y animales asfixiándose de calor, amontonados hasta en el techo de los vagones. Era la fiebre del banano. En veinticuatro horas transformaron el pueblo. 'Me voy', dijo entonces el coronel. 'El olor del banano me descompone los intestinos.' Y abandonó a Macondo en el tren de regreso,... (51)

During the Reyes dictatorship, the Magdalena Department of Colombia became the focus of American capital for the cultivation of bananas. Aracataca (which García Márquez calls Macondo) was one of the towns that enjoyed rapid growth, not only in terms of wealth, but also in the influx of foreigners. When the banana boom declined after the First World War, towns like Aracataca fell into poverty, leaving a mixed community of Colombians and foreigners. Undoubtedly, outsiders spread from Magdalena to neighbouring areas during, or after, the period of prosperity; 'el pueblo' has, for example, the Syrian shopkeepers. Vargas Llosa gives a description of the effects of the banana boom on Northern Colombia (*33*, pp.13-15).

The historical present of the novel, *La Violencia*, is the third point of reference in time. This civil war in Colombia lasted from 1948 until the mid-1960s, claiming the lives of between 200,000 and 300,000 people. Germán Guzmán Campos includes among the major events leading up to *La Violencia* the resounding defeat of the Conservative Government by the Liberals in elections in 1930, after which there followed several years of sectarian violence (*40*, chs 2-3). This was followed in the mid-1940s by a split of the Liberal party into two factions: the followers of Gabriel Turbay, and the supporters of the more populist Jorge Eliécer Gaitán (the ex-mayor of Bogotá and former Minister of Education). On the death of Turbay, the Liberals united behind Gaitán. They were in power until 1946, when a Conservative, Mariano Ospina Pérez, was elected President. He tried to rule by coalition, but the Liberals in the cabinet resigned in March 1948. Unlike other Liberal leaders, Gaitán was a fierce opponent of collaboration with the Conservatives. He was openly murdered in Bogotá on 9 April 1948; by whom and why is still a subject of discussion. The immediate violent reaction of the Liberal mob led to a period of anarchy and murder, known as the Bogotazo.

The *bogotazo* was more than a dramatic outpouring of emotion and unrestrained, bestial violence. With the veneer of civilization stripped away, the entire moral fabric of the nation was revealed in its rotting reality. (*41*, p.59).

It was chiefly the peasants who became involved in the fervour that both sides exploited. Nevertheless, the political leaders washed their hands of the peasant violence, blaming instead illiteracy, sickness, alcoholism and the inadequacy of the people's political education. Not all the country was affected, but Sucre, in the State of Bolívar, was in one of the areas of fighting. *La Violencia* fell into four periods: the first wave of violence, from 1949-53; the truce of 1953, during which Lieutenant-General Gustavo Rojas Pinilla, who became President by a *coup d'état*, offered an amnesty to all guerrillas; a renewed outbreak of fighting between 1954 and 1957, including a Conservative offensive against Liberal strongholds throughout the country; and the 'pausa' of 1958, which was followed by continued but decreasing violence until 1966. By 1956, Rojas' presidency had become a universally unpopular dictatorship (*41*, p.222), and when, in 1957, he declared that his term of office would continue until 1962, the outcry from all sides was so strong, including a joint manifesto by the Liberals and Conservatives, that Rojas was compelled to allow free elections. On 10 May 1957, Rojas handed over to five generals, with the result that a constitutional alternation of power between the two parties was drawn up. The old boundaries between Liberals and Conservatives had been worn away and the first President under this new system was Dr Alberto Lleras Camargo.

In the second wave of violence, the fighting had developed on a number of levels, all involving the peasants. They were persecuted by the army and police, by guerrillas and by counter-guerrillas, and by peasants of the opposite political persuasion. Guzmán points out that the latent aggression in the poor classes stemmed from a lack of social mobility, plus a growing awareness of the extent of the frustration of their aspirations (*40*, p.70). Self-defence groups were formed to promote development, but the leaders of the self-defence movements failed to promote the ideal of taking power, so that the violent dictatorial methods of the oligarchy were aimed at peasants who had no obvious goal.

Social immobility in Colombia has not been limited to the period of *La Violencia*. Alfredo Vázquez Carrizosa, a former Foreign Minister, was quoted in *The International Herald Tribune* of 19 August 1981 (p.1) as saying that 'The characteristic phenomenon of Colombian political life is immobility'. The preliminary list of Presidential candidates for 1982 included three sons of ex-Presidents, as it did in 1974, and many of the powerful families have remained the same since the nineteenth century. It is that immobility that has bred such terrorist movements as M-19,[7] with which Gabriel García Márquez's name was linked in 1981. The accusation was later withdrawn, but the charge and threat of detention for questioning had already forced García Márquez to leave Colombia for Mexico.

What we learn of The War of 1000 Days in the novel is told either through the Colonel's memory and dreams (for instance, of the Treaty of Neerlandia, and of Colonel Aureliano Buendía

---

[7] M-19 is the popular name for the April 19 Guerrilla Movement, one of the most active and well-supported guerrilla groups operating in Colombia since the mid-1970s.

and the Duke of Marlborough, 16),[8] or in relation to the
Colonel's, and his wife's, suffering as a result of bureaucratic
indifference to the many soldiers who (like the Colonel) have
relied on the promise of a pension: 'Todos mis compañeros se
murieron esperando el correo' (28); 'Necesitó medio siglo para
darse cuenta de que no había tenido un minuto de sosiego
después de la rendición de Neerlandia' (51). The war itself is
relatively unimportant compared to the Treaty of Neerlandia
and the guarantees made after it. The Treaty is described thus in
El coronel:

> Había empezado a escucharla al día siguiente del tratado
> de Neerlandia cuando el gobierno prometió auxilios de
> viaje e indemnizaciones a doscientos oficiales de la
> revolución. Acampado en torno a la gigantesca ceiba de
> Neerlandia un batallón revolucionario compuesto en gran
> parte por adolescentes fugados de la escuela, esperó
> durante tres meses. Luego regresaron a sus casas por sus
> propios medios y allí siguieron esperando. (29)

In *Cien años de soledad*, the Treaty appears on pp. 154-57.
García Márquez tells González Bermejo that the treasurer of the
revolutionary forces at Neerlandia, who takes the gold to
Aureliano Buendía, is the Colonel of *El coronel* (*21*, p.18). This
is borne out by the text:

> Como tesorero de la revolución...Llegó al campamento de
> Neerlandia arrastrando la mula muerta de hambre media
> hora antes de que se firmara el tratado. El coronel
> Aureliano Buendía...extendió el recibo de los fondos e

---

[8] García Márquez makes anachronistic use of the Duke of Marlborough from
the rhyme 'Marlborough s'en va-t-en guerre', which became in Spanish:
> Mambrú se fue a la guerra,
> qué dolor, qué dolor,
> qué pena.

See *34*, p.162, *33*, p.109, and *1*, p.xi. Rodríguez Monegal says that the use of the
Duke in *Cien años de soledad* is a cultural metaphor of a great warrior (*30*,
pp.32-33). The Duke also appears in *La hojarasca*, p.120, and 'El mar del tiempo
perdido', where an old revolutionary says the Duke appeared in answer to the
need for a good general (*2*, pp.227-28).

incluyó los dos baúles en el inventario de la rendición. (31)

García Márquez's grandfather, Colonel Nicolás Márquez Iguarán, claimed that he was Intendente for Uribe Uribe (*33*, pp.28 and 110), and he, like the Colonel in *El coronel*, spent his life after the Civil War waiting for the pension that he expected in recognition for his services in the War.

García Márquez has deviated from historical fact regarding Neerlandia, the time scale, and the question of pensions. He never mentions the second Treaty, signed on board the *Wisconsin*, presumably, as Vargas Llosa says, because his grandfather was not there, whereas he did attend the signing at Neerlandia (*33*, p.122). If the book is set in 1956, and also states that is is fifty-six years since the last civil war (3), the Treaty of Neerlandia would have been signed in 1900. Furthermore, the Colonel remembers waiting ten years after the Treaty until the banana company enters Macondo in 1906; by this calculation, the Treaty was signed in 1896. Neither Treaty contains a clause offering financial recognition to the soldiers of either side (*42*, pp.186-90; *38*, pp.186-87; *33*, p.123).

The banana boom, as recalled by the Colonel, is condensed into three sentences, and serves only as the motive for the Colonel's departure from Macondo for 'el pueblo', outside the banana-growing area, where the smell cannot upset his stomach. The reference to Macondo and bananas relates *El coronel* to *La hojarasca*, its predecessor (and to García Márquez's subsequent books), but, more important, it gives a further historical dimension, although in the Colonel's mind it appears to be coupled with the unfulfilled guarantees of Neerlandia. Pontiero takes the 'fiebre del banano' to be yellow fever. By extension, he calls the episode a 'natural disaster', which is only partly true, since bananas and their attendant miseries were introduced by the Americans. However, he rightly adds that the banana boom is equated with the Colonel's 'personal history of decline and futility. When he suddenly awakes, the nightmare is over, but the sense of alienation and disquiet remain' (*1*, p.xxv).

In *El coronel*, no direct description of *La Violencia* as a historical period is given, a fact remarked upon by many critics.

Rafael Conte says that in the concision of the text, the major themes (one being politics) are hinted at, and are only mentioned surreptitiously (*12*, p.169); also, Emir Rodríguez Monegal points out that the political focus is distanced (*30*, p.23). Mario Vargas Llosa, in discussing the theme of politics in *El coronel*, shows how the subject is insinuated in the narrative, by means of 'datos escondidos' and 'cajas chinas' (facts not told by the narrator, but introduced by a character in conversation; *33*, pp.309-13). He says that all political references are short, almost casual, but are made maliciously, and the reason that they are treated like contraband is that, if told bluntly, they would lose their power of persuasion or their objective character. William Rowe makes a similar point: violence is part of everyday life, but since we hear about it through oblique references, it seems normal. This creates a sense of shock and shows how repressive authority tries to make itself appear natural (*32*). An obvious example is '—Este entierro es un acontecimiento—dijo el coronel—. Es el primer muerto de muerte natural que tenemos en muchos años' (7): in one sentence the political violence has been summed up, but indirectly and, as Pontiero says, with a humour that betrays indifference and resignation (*1*, p.75).

Interviews with García Márquez have clarified the author's own attitude towards writing about *La Violencia*. He tells González Bermejo that it was a political decision to write *El coronel* and *La mala hora*, since he felt that he could not write an escapist book of the mythological nature of *Cien años de soledad* during such a tragic period of Colombian history (*21*, pp.21-22; see also *28*, pp.82-84). But unlike most novels about *La Violencia*, which are catalogues of death and methods of torture, García Márquez's books look for the motives and consequences:

> los lectores latinoamericanos, creo yo, no necesitan que les siga contando su propio drama de opresión e injusticia, porque ya lo conocen de sobra en su vida cotidiana, lo sufren en carne propia, y lo que esperan de una novela es que les revele algo nuevo. (*18*, p.64)

What is new in terms of Colombian literature of the mid-twentieth century is that García Márquez concentrates on the people to whose lives violence is a permanent background. The references to political events retain their objectivity because the events are seen as the cause of the state of society in which individuals react, either corruptly or with integrity. In this way, politics do not envelop everyday thoughts and actions. Vargas Llosa also gives García Márquez's attitude towards fictionalizing *La Violencia*, particularly as he expressed it in 'Dos o tres cosas sobre la novela de la violencia': 'la novela no estaba en los muertos...sino en los vivos que debieron sudar hielo en su escondite.' In this, García Márquez admits to following Camus' treatment of the plague in Oran in *La Peste* (*33*, pp.128-32 and p.198). The Colonel suffers in just such a manner: 'También el coronel sufrió una recaída. Agonizó muchas horas en el excusado, sudando hielo, sintiendo que se pudría...' (35).

Angel Rama calls the violence that existed in Colombia for so long a substratum to life, adding that in García Márquez's works, violence and political oppression are 'concomitantes' (*29*, p.64). Rama goes on to say that *El coronel* and *La mala hora* should be read as one novel, in order to gain an overall impression of a Colombian town during *La Violencia*. Ernesto Volkening compares the treatment of politics in the two novels, saying that in *El coronel* it is peripheral, while in *La mala hora* it is far more significant, the town becoming the worst town of all.[9] Continuing the link between *El coronel* and *La mala hora*, Rodríguez Monegal compares the mayor in *La mala hora* with the Colonel, saying that the mayor (also seen very briefly in *El coronel*) represents power paralysed by its own lust for more power, while the Colonel represents the other side of the coin: an opposition to repressive forces immobilised in its beginnings by the mockery of the Treaty of Neerlandia by successive Governments (*30*, p.23).

The theme of politics is a strong unifying element in the novel. Everyone, rich or poor, forgetful of it or not, in opposition to it

[9] 'A propósito de *La mala hora*', in *Homenaje a Gabriel García Márquez*, pp.87-96, at p.91. The original title of *La mala hora* was 'Este pueblo de mierda', a phrase that Don Sabas uses on p.42 of *El coronel*.

or not, is subject to the state of siege in force in 1956. The repression resulting from *La Violencia* causes some of the social conditions described; others (such as the Colonel's poverty) are caused by an earlier political upheaval. Therefore, politics provide the historical reference for the novel, and the two civil wars are linked by the life of the central character. The Colonel fought in The War of 1000 Days as a revolutionary; there are a number of references to his political involvement between that time and the present of the novel:

> Lo había ganado la mujer en una tómbola política destinada a recolectar fondos para el partido del coronel.(5)

> Se acordó de los dirigentes de su partido, escrupulosamente peinados, abanicándose en el patio de su casa al compás de la música. (66)

and, despite his cynicism, he is still involved in clandestine activities. His son was similarly involved during the early years of *La Violencia*, but was machine-gunned to death as a consequence.[10] The Colonel's life, and specifically three months of it, is the central focus in the narrative, so that the first civil war is seen via his memory, and its end as the cause of his misery. The second, *La Violencia*, is the source of the social privations and corruption around him, plus the further misery of the loss of his son.

References to the fictional past of the novel also appear in memories or dreams or in dialogue, and many detailed dates are given: 7 April 1922, the birth of Agustín, in the same year as the birth of the dead musician (4); when Agustín was eight (i.e. 1930), the Colonel and his wife won a circus umbrella in a political fund-raising tombola (5-6); 12 August 1949, when the Colonel was included on the register (33); 1931, when the Colonel's wife last went to the cinema (34); 3 January 1956, the

---

[10]Agustín's death in the cockpit (on 3 January, 1956) is an echo of the Bull-Ring Massacre of 5 February, 1956 in which opponents of President Rojas who did not cheer him at a bull-fight were beaten up; eight people were killed, fifty injured.

death of Agustín (37); 2.18 p.m., Wednesday, 27 June 1906, when the Colonel left Macondo (51). The specific dates in the past show the intensity of the memories of the Colonel and his wife, clarified by their present hunger and misery. Similarly the date of the cockfight to come is given exactly, 20 January at 3 p.m. (71). Days of hope, joy or despair are noted with precision, but not so the passing years. We have seen above how the period of time since the Treaty of Neerlandia is confused twice. In much the same way, there is uncertainty over the order of events of the past twenty years. On pp.26-27 is the following statement:

> Diecinueve años antes, cuando el congreso promulgó la ley, se inició un proceso de justificación que duró ocho años. Luego necesitó seis años más para hacerse incluir en el escalafón. Ésa fue la última carta que recibió el coronel.

That is to say that the law was announced in 1937, which roughly ties in with the twenty years of memories (since requiring a lawyer, 30), and twenty years of waiting (50). Next it took eight years for his claim to be substantiated,[11] that is 1945, and then six more years, until 1951, for him to be included in the register, and that was the date of his last letter. 1951 concurs with the reference to the publication of the last pension list five years ago (16). However, on p.33, we are told that the Colonel was put on the register on 12 August 1949. Also, on p.13 and p.26, the period given for waiting for a letter is fifteen years, which means that the last one came in 1941. In order to account for fifteen years of waiting for a letter, Castagnino subtracts the eight years from 1949, leaving the date 1941. In his calculations he does not mention 'Diecenueve años antes', nor 'Luego necesitó seis años más' (*11*, p.66); it is after these six years that the last letter arrived, not after the eight years of substantiation. It seems that Castagnino has got his figures wrong, which may be what García Márquez did too. Alternatively, the mistakes may be deliberate, showing that the Colonel and his wife have lost track of time, which is unlikely since their memory for other

[11] See *1*, p.30, note 41 on the translation of 'justificación'.

dates is clear enough. Also, when they forget something, it is usually of the immediate future: the musician's funeral, tomorrow being Friday, the cockfight trials. Nevertheless, it cannot be denied that the frequency of references to the number of years of waiting, to phases of life ('cuarenta años de vida común', 49), to rituals (going for the mail every Friday; 'Estás diciendo lo mismo desde hace quince años', 69), to outside events ('Es un circo—dijo—. Es el primero que viene en diez años', 64), emphasises the scale of their frustration.

Time within the narrative is a device to show the linear nature of the story. A detailed analysis reveals that the timespan of each chapter varies; the following outline is illustrative, not exhaustive. Chapter 1 deals with one morning in October: at 7.20 a.m. the Colonel winds the clock (5); after 9 a.m. the weather clears up. Chapter 2 moves from Thursday (12), through Friday (the mail day) to after 6 p.m. on Saturday (20) of the following week. During the following week (Chapter 3, 23), Monday to Friday is mentioned either directly or indirectly ('la tarde', 'la segunda tarde', 'miércoles', 23; 'jueves en la noche', 'al día siguiente esperó las lanchas', i.e. Friday, 24); by p.26 it is 'El viernes siguiente', leading up to Saturday evening. In Chapter 4, the pace is increased a little: 27 October (33), 2 November (35), the second fortnight of November (36), in which we hear of one unspecified afternoon and evening. Chapter 5 takes place one month after they have changed lawyers (44), two months after the musician's funeral (47). In Chapter 6 we are told only that it is Sunday, but midday, the siesta, evening and night are mentioned. Also in this chapter references concentrate on hours and minutes: 'diez minutos', 'veinte minutos' (52), 'quiso haber llegado una hora más tarde' (56), and 'El coronel sintió pasar los cinco segundos más largos de su vida' (53). At this point, the Colonel is at his lowest ebb: he is about to sell the cock and betray his convictions so that all the long years of waiting for his pension contain less importance than these five seconds. Later in this chapter, as Pontiero notes, time slows again to a ponderous rhythm when the Colonel leaves Don Sabas's office and walks through the 'pueblo paralizado' (54; see *1*, p.xxiv). Since Don Sabas is preoccupied with business, and then goes away, the Colonel has time by Chapter 7 to change his mind about the sale. With the arrival of December he is strong again, as we see from breakfast-time on Friday to dawn on Sunday, 8 December (the previous day it was 44 days to 20 January; 71).

There are direct references to time, allusions to it (meal-times, the curfew bugle, cock crow, Mass), and spoken references: 'Tienes media hora de estar molestando a mi compadre con tus tonterías' (44-45). Also, on numerous occasions, there are expressions of immediacy: 'en ese momento', 'en ese instante', 'un momento después', 'entonces', 'sólo entonces', often used with verbs such as 'advertir', 'descubrir', or 'acordar'; expressions of simultaneity: 'mientras', 'durante', of ritual: 'cada vez que', 'como siempre', 'a la rutina', and of suspense: 'en suspenso' (29, 53). The smallest elements are important for revealing character (forgetfulness) or the way in which everyday life can yield surprises. But of much greater significance is the contrast between the small and large temporal elements. The gaps between the months, weeks and days alter the pace of the narrative, but time leads inevitably to a point where the Colonel has to make a decision. In contrast to this passage of time, his waiting (and that of everybody in the town—for political change, improved conditions), which has lasted so long, makes time appear static (*1*, p.xxx; *37*, p.288). It is the sudden revelations, the drudgery of routine, or of suspense, expressed in the short phrases, that highlight the immobility and lethargy that pervade each day.

References to the future, beyond the scope of the narrative, provide further suspense: three months until the cockfight (36); forty-four days until the cockfight (71); Don Sabas will be away until next Thursday (56), or until Monday (68). Although it is immaterial whether Don Sabas returns or not (because the Colonel changes his mind about selling the cock), the reader is not told the outcome of the cockfight, so he or she must imagine it, and continue to suffer the Colonel's agony of expectation.

Richard D. Woods describes time as expressed in *El coronel* as a 'scaffolding on which to construct the theme of futility' (*37*, p.288). The futility lies in the fact that the static present is merely a repetition of the past (*37*, p.295). All that the Colonel can be sure of is that each year October and its misery, and eventually death, will arrive. Woods also describes time as a spiral, with, as its outer circle, the past, the greatest unit of time; the second circle is the present, refined to months, weeks (with Friday as their axis), hours and minutes, and the core of the spiral is the future, which brightens the present. The concept of a spiral suggests a continuous progression which is not how time is presented. Through the Colonel's, and his wife's, memory and anticipation, all aspects of time are interlocked: there is free movement between all three.

All the time scales are united on page 73:

> El coronel necesitó setenta y cinco años—los setenta y cinco años de su vida, minuto a minuto—para llegar a ese instante. Se sintió puro, explícito, invencible, en el momento de responder:
> —Mierda.

Here the past and present (from seventy-five years to that very instant), and the future (regarding how they will keep alive until the cockfight), vindicate the Colonel's clarity of purpose. Doris Rolfe says that the repetition of temporal expressions in this paragraph makes each example carry implicit in it the force of the previous example so that the Colonel becomes fully aware of his position. He is no longer innocent or stoic, nor is he merely surviving, but he is lucid (*31*, pp.342-43). He also retains his dignity which is seen against physical ruin and moral decline, caused by remote events which, as Graciela Maturo says, García Márquez is denouncing; he is accusing the authors of a treaty that shamed his country and is taking sides against political corruption and social injustice (*26*, p.114).

3 *Character*

In his discussion of *El coronel* Eyzaguirre makes two points about the main character: first, the Colonel is described with economy and psychological subtlety, and second, that as a character, he fails in exterior presentation (*17*, pp. 324 and 330 respectively). In the text, the physical description of the Colonel is subordinate to his emotions, but rather than being a failing, this is a deliberate authorial decision.

After the first chapter, there is no new information given on the appearance of the Colonel except as an extension of what is told in the first few pages. It can also be said that there is little description of his physique that does not have a psychological connotation. The second paragraph illustrates these points:

> Mientras esperaba a que hirviera la infusión, sentado junto a la hornilla de barro cocido en una actitud de confiada e inocente expectativa, el coronel experimentó la sensación de que nacían hongos y lirios venenosos en sus tripas...Octubre era una de las pocas cosas que llegaban. (3)

His attitude, besides suggesting what the Colonel looks like, also points to his nature: trusting, expecting the best, and apparently innocent, which arouses criticisms of *naïveté*. The sensation of fungus and poisonous flowers growing in his stomach is a common image; it is the Colonel's physical reaction to the winter weather, and it echoes the rot that he and his wife see around them. It also emphasises, through suffering (as does his wife's asthma), their misery of hunger and poverty. The Colonel is old, more than fifty-six; we learn later that he is seventy-five and how the majority of those years have been spent, extending the phrase in this paragraph, 'el coronel no había hecho nada distinto de esperar'.

The effect of the oppressive October weather on his body and mind points to his age: he sleeps with his socks on (4); he is forgetful of immediate things (4); he finds it an effort to do things, 'Le costó trabajo encontrarlo' (5), repeated on p.55 and suggested by his shortness of breath (37). In the first chapter his age is also shown in the age spots on his skin, 'Los huesos de sus manos estaban forrados por un pellejo lúcido y tenso, manchado de carate como la piel del cuello' (6).

His bones are important: 'Era un hombre árido, de huesos sólidos articulados a tuerca y tornillo' (7), but, owing to malnutrition, his bones are not covered by much flesh, 'Apoyó en el hueso del muslo la mano derecha — puros huesos cosidos con fibras nerviosas—' (29), which fact later becomes a joke:

—Estás en el hueso pelado—dijo.
—Me estoy cuidando para venderme—dijo el coronel—.
Ya estoy encargado por una fábrica de clarinetes. (36)

In reality, though, his bones are 'molidos por la vigilia' (36). His bones also tell him when December has arrived (62). The Colonel's hair, like his joints, is metallic (7), which, when cut, makes him feel twenty years younger (23). The other parts of the Colonel's body that are described are his eyes (which have special significance, to be discussed below), 'Por la vitalidad de sus ojos no parecía conservado en formol' (7), and his teeth, mentioned in the phrases 'Apretó los dientes' and 'con los dientes apretados'. Since these phrases are used at times when the Colonel is under some form of pressure, they retain the traditional meaning of struggle, and emphasise the Colonel's resolve: at the musician's funeral (8), asking the doctor for a bill (19), asking for credit (35), before talking to Don Sabas about the cock (53), telling Don Sabas, in front of the doctor, that he is going to sell the cock (57), when confronted with the policeman (61).

Gritting his teeth is one of the Colonel's habitual actions; others are trying to relieve constipation, waiting for the letter and going for the mail, always putting clandestine leaflets in his trouser pocket (19, 39, 60), trusting in the victory of the cock. Such rituals characterise him, compared with the majority of characters whose physical description is even more schematic (see pp.52 and 84 below). However, there is one aspect that complements the scantness of physical description and underlines the importance of his emotions, his anonymity. In the first place, the Colonel has no name. To this is added the impression that he has no face because he never looks at himself:

> Después de afeitarse al tacto—pues carecía de espejo desde hacía mucho tiempo— (6)

> Trató de acordar sus movimientos a los de la imagen.
> —Se las comen los puercos—dijo ella...
> Buscó a la mujer en el espejo y se dio cuenta de que continuaba con la misma expresión. Al resplandor del fuego su rostro parecía modelado en la materia de la hornilla. Sin advertirlo, fijos los ojos en ella, el coronel siguió afeitándose al tacto como lo había hecho durante muchos años. (62-63)

When 'Se vio a sí mismo con su mujer y su hijo' (66), it is in a memory of 'otra época'. In the past, before martial law, he was an important figure, and he recalls himself as such. In the present he is just one of many oppressed Colombians, therefore his name and what he looks like are unimportant, but how he copes with what oppresses him is vital. His ritual actions are not meaningless, they give him strength; 'Hacía cada cosa como si fuera un acto trascendental' (6). As William Rowe says, he makes every action count in order to survive (*32*).

It is not only actions that are transcendental: 'Excitado por los recuerdos asumió una actitud trascendental' (29; N.B. there is a misprint in *1* here: 'transcendental' for 'trascendental', see Plaza y Janés edition, p.47, and Sudamericana edition, p.38). The keenness inspired by memory here gives him strength to tell his lawyer that he has decided to terminate his contract. The memory of political freedom is instrumental in his decision to keep the cock; he transposes the people's enthusiasm for the cock into expectations of future political liberalisation (66). As Rowe again says, his memory of how things were fortifies him, as does his view that what he stands for matters for everybody

(*32*). What he does and remembers gives him defiant energy, to make an effort for his own sake to overcome the numbing effect of static time and the winter weather, and for everybody's sake to return to a more favourable political system.

The Colonel's anonymity and his strength of character are emphasised when he says, 'El gallo no se vende', and his wife follows him into the bedroom; 'Lo sintió completamente humano, pero inasible, como si lo estuviera viendo en la pantalla de un cine' (67). Compare this with her chiding:

> —Lo que pasa es que a ti te falta carácter—dijo luego—. Te presentas como si fueras a pedir una limosna cuando debías llegar con la cabeza levantada y llamar aparte a mi compadre y decirle: 'Compadre, he decidido venderle el gallo.' (54)

Before he has decided to sell the cock, he is characterless to his wife; afterwards, although she finds him flat and unapproachable, he is completely human. The image of the cinema screen portrays the distance that has grown between the two protagonists (it also refers to the author's literary technique; see chapter 5 below). Furthermore, it is ironic that his wife should find him human when he is resolved not to do what she wants, while previously, when he was wavering and could possibly accede to her demands, he was without character. He infuriates her because his resolve expresses itself in stoicism and inactivity, which is why she says, 'Eres caprichoso, terco y desconsiderado...Toda una vida comiendo tierra para que ahora resulte que merezco menos consideración que un gallo' (70).

His apparent resignation hides a wide range of emotions. Regarding the possibility of a letter coming, he feels 'una ansiedad muy distinta pero tan apremiante como el terror', then he feels 'avergonzado' when there is none (14). On a later occasion, 'sintió el terror' followed by 'defraudado' (26). Among other negative emotions are 'desconcertado' (9), 'se alarmó' (31), 'desgraciado' (38), 'Al coronel se le embrollaban las ideas' (38), which can be linked with his wonder at aeroplane travel (24) and at the sheer size of nine hundred pesos (45). He feels intimidated by crowds (66). He is 'contagiado de un humor sombrío' (47), bitter (49) and offended and humiliated (50) at his poverty and especially at having to hide it. Having slept in Don Sabas' office, he feels ashamed (52) and, waiting for Don Sabas, he feels 'impaciente' (53). He is often convincing himself, justifying things to himself (34, 57), and he lies.

On the positive side, he is gentle with his sick wife (37) and feels sympathy for her when he thinks she is lying (47). In the same vein, 'El coronel sufrió con la idea de haber sido injusto' (30), and he feels ashamed at having caused Álvaro to bet wrongly at roulette (61); in both instances, his self-criticism is unjustified. He is forward-looking: 'El coronel había previsto aquel momento' (36). He does not despair at all times, for instance when waiting for Don Sabas, 'No se desesperó a pesar de que no había previsto ese contratiempo' (63). Although he is at times disconsolate, he does not lack humour. He is contemplative, 'rumiando las revelaciones del médico' (60). He is acutely observant: 'Hasta donde alcanzaba su vista el pueblo estaba tapizado de flores' (7); 'siguió con un irresistible sentimiento de culpa el rastrillo de madera que arrastró el dinero de Álvaro' (61); 'El coronel observó la confusión de rostros cálidos, ansiosos, terriblemente vivos' (65). His most keen observation is reserved for the arrival of the post launch and the movements of the administrator (13, 24-25, 64); he knows the process so well that he can easily recall it, 'Pensó en el administrador de correos saltando a la lancha con un impermeable de hule' (44). His powers of observation are as important to him as his transcendental actions.

The Colonel is also passive: 'El coronel no experimentó ninguna emoción' (65); he watches Don Sabas's wife 'con una mirada completamente inconsciente' (52); 'permaneció inmóvil' (54); 'El coronel no movió un músculo' when his wife rebuffs him (50). But his passivity becomes calm self-assertion in other confrontations:

> Y entonces vio de cerca, por la primera vez en su vida, al hombre que disparó contra su hijo. Estaba exactamente frente a él con el cañón del fusil apuntando contra su

vientre...El coronel apretó los dientes y apartó suavemente
con la punta de los dedos el cañón del fusil.
—Permiso—dijo. (61)
Entonces saltó la barrera, se abrió paso a través de la
multitud concentrada en el redondel y se enfrentó a los
tranquilos ojos de Germán. Se miraron sin parpadear. (65)

Many of the emotions in these three general types (negative,
positive, contemplative/passive) reinforce his integrity. We have
seen above that his observation and habitual actions foster
defiant energy which in turn fuels his strength of character. To
the people around him, this is invisible, and, to the same extent,
his integrity, which is based on intangible things, is not revealed
to others.

Emmanuel Carballo puts the Colonel's struggle on two levels,
the superficial fight to survive humiliation, and 'la lucha sin
cuartel y sin tregua que sostiene el hombre contra el transcurrir
del tiempo'. He fights age, illness and 'la postergación de su
persona'.[12] Eyzaguirre calls it the Hispanoamerican trait of
retaining integrity in the face of the impossibility of changing
things (*17*, p.328), while Ariza González says, more
dramatically, that the Colonel is like a lone fighter against a
bloody and uncommon enemy (*7*, p.23). Vargas Llosa regards
the confrontation between the Colonel's idealistic optimism and
the brutality of the outside world as the dramatic conflict of the
novel (*33*, p.321). The Colonel appears weak: he loiters at the
dock, he seems directionless in Don Sabas's office (42, 52-54),
people tell him what to do (his wife, the tailor's apprentices; 39).
The humiliation of poverty and of having outlived his political
usefulness does not deprive him totally of deferential treatment
from others, but that does not prevent the doctor calling him
politically naïve (15, 59), or the apprentices calling him 'bobo'
(39). However, Dorfman says that the Colonel is pathetic only in
other people's eyes (*15*, p.123). His political attitudes are based
on his memories of a past democracy, and a basic trust in people
(even though some, like Don Sabas, show themselves to be

[12] Emmanuel Carballo, 'Un gran novelista latinoamericano', in *Sobre García
Márquez*, pp.68-77, at p.71.

undeserving). Basic trust, and faith in something good eventually turning up, are part of the self-respect that reveals itself as weakness. Being prepared to wait means reliving weekly a painful experience, putting up with humiliation. This is founded on an unwillingness to surrender. He was opposed to Colonel Aureliano Buendía's surrendering (35), an action which has led to his own suffering. His own and his son's opposition to the Government resulted in Agustín's death and his continued suffering. His decision not to sell the cock, despite a decline in hopes of a letter coming, ensures further hardship. Never giving in is a form of pride which is more obvious in 'Ya estoy cansado de andar pidiendo favores' (34), and in his refusal to wear a hat (57) or to borrow an umbrella (8, 42).

His unprotected head is a milder form of self-sacrifice than the suffering that never yielding brings, but self-sacrifice also inspires lies:

> Pero se incorporó para recibir la taza.
> —Y tú—dijo.
> —Ya tomé—mintió el coronel. Todavía quedaba una cucharada grande. (3)

To others, his pride appears as stubbornness, which is a superficial reaction to his desire to retain his dignity. It is ironic, however, that people's appreciation of the Colonel should be superficial when he himself is concerned about his appearance: '—Debo parecer un papagayo—dijo' (7); 'Si me ven por la calle con semejante escaparate me sacan en una canción de Rafael Escalona' (38); and less ashamedly, but still conscious of being a subject of attention, 'El coronel se sintió intimidado. Volvió a abrirse paso, sin mirar a nadie, aturdido por los aplausos y los gritos, y salió a la calle con el gallo bajo el brazo.' Even a black charlatan loses his audience when 'Todo el pueblo—la gente de abajo—salió a verlo pasar seguido por los niños de la escuela' (66). On this occasion he does not repent of making a spectacle of himself; not only has he brought the town to life, he has reached a positive decision about the cock. It is not vanity but self-esteem that makes him want to be seen to act according to his principles.

Another important element is his humour, at times spontaneous ('Los gallos se gastan de tanto mirarlos', 5; 'Eres idéntica al hombrecito de la avena Quaker', 55; see *1*, p.xii), at others resigned, falling back on clichés ('Esto empieza a parecerse al cuento del gallo capón', 28; 'El que espera lo mucho espera lo poco', 32). As William Rowe says, the Colonel's use of humour is a refusal to accept things as they are because he takes the clichés literally (see Chapter 5 below). To his wife, though, his spontaneous humour seems like avoiding the issues, and to others, clichés may appear an unimaginative response to difficulties.

The most important things, says Vargas Llosa, take place in the Colonel's mind (*33*, p.321). While it is true that what he does not say is more significant than what he says when it is a question of hiding true emotions (*17*, p.324; see also Chapter 5 below), there are occasions when his silence appears as yet another case of pride. For instance, on only one visit to the post wharf does the Colonel ask directly if there is a letter (46); on page 14 the postman tells him, on page 26 the doctor asks on his behalf. The Colonel tries hard, as Brushwood comments, to hide the fact that he is hopeful.[13] When he lies, 'No esperaba nada...Yo no tengo quien me escriba' (14), he is transparent; why has he been going to the dock each Friday for fifteen years? He does not tell Don Sabas or the apprentices the real reason for wanting to be rid of the cock (either for sale, or to let them feed it). He never actually tells the lawyer why he wants to change. Not that there is any need for him to explain himself: Don Sabas shows some understanding, but little sympathy, for the Colonel's position (45, 58), Germán realises his predicament (41), as does the lawyer. While he does support his wife by asking for credit and lying about his financial prospects (35), he cannot lose face by asking for hard cash, unlike her (she even tries to pawn their wedding rings).

The difference between the Colonel's exterior demeanour and his inner strengths is summed up in the image 'El coronel con su manera de andar habitual que parecía la de un hombre que

---

[13] John S. Brushwood, *The Spanish American Novel: A Twentieth-Century Survey* (Austin: University of Texas Press, 1975), p.218.

desanda el camino para buscar una moneda perdida' (15). He appears physically hunched, bowed under the strain of living. There is a suggestion of carelessness at having lost money, and poverty at having to look for it. The image is echoed later when his wife says, 'Te presentas como si fueras a pedir una limosna' (54). On the other hand, the first image recalls his treasurership of the revolution and having to give up the funds (*26*, p.111). There is also a hint of the hope of returning to better times and regaining prosperity.

Besides the contrast between the appearance and the spirit of the Colonel, there are also contrasts within his character, recognised by many critics: 'Childlike in his candour, he is at the same time profoundly wise, and utterly resolute in his decision to rectify the past' (*1*, p.ix). Harss calls him a sort of aged baby, a withered wonder child, wise and silly, touching and human, enchanted and misguided by life (*23*, p.326). Rolfe says that he has infantile innocence and stoic resistance (*31*, p.338), while Rowe compares his childlike openness with his spirit of defiance (*32*).

The main problem for critics appears to be whether, by the time the Colonel says the final word, he has changed. Does he retain or abandon his hope? McMurray regards 'mierda' as a complete surrender to frustration and despair; nevertheless he is defiant ('puro, explícito, invencible', 73). 'The colonel bears a certain resemblance to the absurd hero, i.e., the protagonist whose passion for life enables him to struggle unceasingly against overwhelming odds.' He emerges triumphant knowing that the struggle equals grandeur, even though he is bound to lose (*23*, p.25). Castagnino, on the other hand, says that the Colonel is immutable throughout the novel (the only character who is) and that his final word is 'a la vez, profunda desesperanza y renacimiento de una hipotética nueva ilusión' (*11*, p.179). Rolfe argues that through a series of self-discoveries, the Colonel reaches final lucidity, which is also a defeat of his hopes (*31*, p.349). Conte believes he finally accepts poverty and hunger, but is loyal to his dreams, while Pontiero sees defiance with an awareness of the hopelessness of his situation, adding that the uncharacteristic outburst of anger 'falls short of any explanation' (*12*, p.170, and *1*, p.xv respectively). Years of waiting for a letter and the annual torture of winter weather almost make the Colonel choose the easy option of cash in hand. Then, on a December Friday when the weather is better, he reasserts himself by breaking a ritual. Instead of going for the post, he shifts his focus of attention away from the letter of the first civil war, onto the cock that is the legacy of his dead son and the present political strife. He recognises the people's feelings towards the bird and he is redirected onto the old struggle of retaining his own values, which now encompasses the brutal present.

Herein lies the Colonel's tragedy. In continuing to fight although realising the hopelessness of his struggle, he remains isolated. As Bollettino says, the tragedy emanates not from direct conflict between the protagonist and other characters, but from the protagonist confronting both a society which does not accept his values and the incessant persecution of fate. It is what Bollettino calls a modern tragedy of social conflict in which man transgresses social norms and therefore reality.[14] According to Dario Carrillo, however, this non-conformity causes isolation, fixing the Colonel in the Hispanoamerican literary theme of solitude (*13*, pp.34-38). Suzanne Jill Levine calls it a general Western theme.[15] It is not a question of the Colonel merely being an outsider or misfit, although at the outset that is how he appears: at the musician's funeral when all the men are dressed in white with black ties (8), the Colonel is in black with no tie (5-6). In his fight to retain his integrity, he refuses to succumb to the corruption around him, but he will not admit that this

[14] Vincenzo Bollettino, 'El concepto trágico en *La hojarasca* de Gabriel García Márquez', *Hispanófila*, no. 53 (January, 1975), 49-59, at pp.49-50. Dario Carrillo remarks on Sophoclean hints in *El coronel*, saying that the Colonel, like Oedipus, 'intuía, y tal vez conocía o re-conocía su sino trágico, pero que, sin embargo, no hizo ni quiso hacer nada que pudiera alterarlo' (*13*, p.15). He adds that in Greek tragedy the essential conflict was between man and the gods or fate, while in *El coronel*, the protagonist's fight is against reality, something tangible.

[15] *El espejo hablado: un estudio de 'Cien años de soledad'* (Caracas: Monte Ávila Editores, 1975), pp.40-41. See also *15*, p.134, where Dorfman refers to the theme of man within time, as a part of history, as a Latin American literary theme. Although his remarks are about *Cien años de soledad*, they are relevant also to *El coronel*.

isolates him:

> Ahora todo el mundo tiene su vida asegurada y tú estás
> muerto de hambre, completamente solo.
> —No estoy solo—dijo el coronel. (71)

His inability to explain himself to his wife is the solitude arising
from a failure to communicate. Just as his strength of will to
keep the cock is too deep-rooted to put into words, so his
waiting for a pension was founded on a natural desire to expect
his right. Contrary to what he says to his wife, he has, in the
course of the novel, become aware of his solitude:

> —La unión hace la fuerza.
> —En este caso no la hizo—dijo el coronel, por primera vez
> dándose cuenta de su soledad—. Todos mis compañeros se
> murieron esperando el correo. (28)

It is the loneliness of 'tratando de esperar una pensión que nunca
llega' (González Bermejo, *21*, p.18; see also Gullón, *22*, p.156).
There is a marked difference between the final scene of the
novel, when the Colonel and his wife each sound unyielding in
their unwillingness to understand the other's point of view, and
the more gentle opening when the Colonel takes his wife her
breakfast coffee in bed. In the early stages of the story, their
marriage is seen as caring: the Colonel deprives himself of coffee
so that his wife can have some, they share reminiscences, his
wife regards him with affection. When the Colonel finds some
humour in his appearance ('Debo parecer un papagayo'; 7), his
wife says that he does not. Of this denial Pontiero says:

> The man she sees before her is no figure of fun but the
> brave young hero who fought for the ideals he cherished.
> In the old woman's eyes, her husband is a man too honest
> and proud for his times and she finds his stoic attitude to
> the injustices they have suffered altogether exasperating.
> (*1*, p.xiii)

His view takes into account her earlier recognition of how much he has aged since their wedding (6). Nevertheless, she is not averse to seeing him with a sense of fun: 'Extendió una camisa fabricada con género de tres colores diferentes, salvo el cuello y los puños que eran del mismo color—. En los carnavales te bastará con quitarte el saco' (20). In their suffering, ill health and mourning their dead son, they support each other. Pontiero says that their marriage remains secure and meaningful throughout the novel, regardless of 'However serious the problems...and however stormy the moments of friction, provoked by a sense of desperation rather than any deep-rooted antagonism' (*1*, p.xviii). Castagnino, on the other hand, considers that the wife changes in the middle of Chapter 3 from being a passive ally to the Colonel to being provocative (*11*, p.84). The first sign of this is before their discussion over changing lawyers:

'Ya hemos cumplido con esperar', le dijo esa noche su mujer. 'Se necesita tener esa paciencia de buey que tú tienes para esperar una carta durante quince años.' (26)

They argue in the fourth, fifth and seventh chapters, the final confrontation showing how uncomprehending each is of the other's point of view. In Castagnino's opinion, the Colonel's wife's attempt to pawn their wedding rings (49) is a symbol of the final breakdown of their marriage contract (*11*, p.100).

Castagnino's argument is based upon the premise that each character is a function within the text, which may well remove subjective criteria from criticism, but also narrows the scope of the couple's relationship in the novel. The Colonel's wife does become provocative, causing her husband to decide to change lawyers, to try to sell the clock, consider selling the cock, and possibly contributing to his eventual resolve to keep the bird, but this does not alienate the Colonel from his wife. While writing the letter, he leaves the door open in case he has to consult her (33). He suggests that they can go to the cinema when the money arrives (34). He is gentle with her when she is ill (37). His joke about her looking like the Quaker Oats man is also gentle although she does not appreciate it (55); similarly, his joke that God is on his side (51). When he thinks that she is lying, he tries to console her because he understands how she is suffering (47, 49). For her part, when planning what to buy with Don Sabas' money, the essentials include a new pair of shoes and a shaving mirror for her husband (55). On hearing that her plans may not come to fruition, she is not angry with the Colonel; she does feel resentment, but also shame (55).

In the final chapter, the old woman appears almost entirely antagonistic. In contrast to the Colonel feeling well now that December has arrived, she shouts at the children and calls the cock a bird of ill omen (62); she follows the Colonel's urging her to sow roses, and his joke about fattening pigs, with a negative and expressionless response (62-63); she upbraids her husband for not wearing his new shoes (63). As the chapter progresses, the Colonel finds himself 'perseguido por la voz frenética de la mujer' (67). Her replies are antithetical or complaining, and, even in silence, the Colonel 'se sabía amenazado por la vigilia de la mujer' (71). She talks at him implacably, accusing him of failing in the past to gain what was rightfully his (71). When he is asleep she talks at him, and when he is awake she accepts not one of his suggestions. His indifference to her continual questioning leads her to shake him physically (73). The Colonel's answer as to what they should eat is not what she wants to hear. To her mind, the only solution is to sell the cock, for without money they cannot survive. The final confrontation between the wife's pragmatism and the Colonel's idealism points to a degeneration in their secure relationship and does not bode well for the future.

This contrast of outlook between the main protagonists is apparent throughout the book. His wife is always urging the Colonel to act, she tries to sell their goods herself, and her practicality in cooking and mending contrasts with the Colonel's inactivity and reliance on illusions. On the passage:

—Lo que pasa es que a ti te falta carácter—dijo luego—. Te presentas como si fueras a pedir una limosna cuando debías llegar con la cabeza levantada y llamar aparte a mi compadre y decirle: 'Compadre, he decidido venderle el gallo.'

Así la vida es un soplo—dijo el coronel. (54)

Suzanne Jill Levine says, 'No sólo esto revela el contraste entre
los hombres y las mujeres de García Márquez sino también la
actitud de admiración del hombre por la fuerza de la mujer.'[16]
The difference between men and women to which she refers is
underlined by Harss, that men are flighty, fanciful creatures,
governed by illusions, while women are solid, sensible,
unvarying paragons of order and stability (*23*, p.327; see also *35*,
pp.172-75, and *28*, p.155). This may indeed be true of Úrsula
Iguarán in *Cien años de soledad*, but as Pontiero points out,
there are only glimpses of the woman as refuge or paragon of
stability in the Colonel's wife (*1*, p.xvii). These glimpses (putting
the house in new order, 17, 54; she would sing if Agustín's
mourning year was up, 18) occur on her recovery from the
asthmatic attacks which contribute so fiercely and debilitatingly
to her suffering, which she describes: 'Debías darte cuenta de
que me estoy muriendo, que esto que tengo no es una
enfermedad sino una agonía' (70).

When she is well, Pontiero adds, she quips to the doctor, 'Un
día de éstos me muero y me lo llevo a los infiernos' (19), and to
her husband, 'Cuando estoy bien soy capaz de resucitar un
muerto' (24). Her jokes revolve around her preoccupation with
death, which is the emotional equivalent of her physical
characterisation, her asthmatic breathing. It has of course been
intensified by the death of her son, whose memory is brought
back by the dead musician (3-4). 'Pensó en el muerto' (3) and
'cerró los ojos para pensar más intensamente en el muerto' (6).
She prevents her husband putting the light out because 'No
quiero morirme en las tinieblas' (71). The meaning of death for
her is tied to their suffering: when, on pages 50 and 71, she tells
the Colonel that he is dying of hunger, the same applies to her.
When death comes, they will have nothing to show for their lives
unless the Colonel acts (by selling the cock). 'The mystery of
death', says Pontiero, 'is ever present in this old woman's
thoughts — the waste and futility of death on the one hand, the

[16] *El espejo hablado*, p.34.

Christian view of its inevitability and acceptance on the other'
(*1*, p.xvii). This is in comparison with her husband's
unwillingness to face the stark reality of their predicament:

> —Es por la situación en que estamos—dijo—. Es pecado
> quitarnos el pan de la boca para echárselo a un gallo. El
> coronel le secó la frente con la sábana.
> —Nadie se muere en tres meses.
> —Y mientras tanto qué comemos—preguntó la mujer.
> —No sé—dijo el coronel—. Pero si nos fuéramos a morir
> de hambre ya nos hubiéramos muerto. (37)

The religious faith of the Colonel's wife can be seen in the
above quotation and on the occasions in which she says the
rosary (33, 49, 50, 68) and the Angelus (20). Her faith does not
exclude jokes, sayings or superstitions ('resucitar un muerto',
24; 'La cara del santo hace el milagro', 56; 'Cruzó los cubiertos
sobre el plato, pero en seguida rectificó supersticiosamente la
posición', 70), but, unlike her husband who also makes religious
jokes (meals being like the multiplication of the loaves and her
coiffeur being like sung mass, 23), she is constant in her faith. It
does not save her from bitterness, though, seen in expressions
such as 'Nosotros somos huérfanos de nuestro hijo' (13), 'Ya ni
siquiera me acuerdo de los monicongos' (34), 'Veinte años
esperando los pajaritos de colores que te prometieron después de
cada elección y de todo eso nos queda un hijo muerto' (50), and
'Todo el mundo ganará con el gallo, menos nosotros' (71).

Although it may not appear so to her, the Colonel tries to
understand his wife:

> El coronel comprobó que cuarenta años de vida común, de
> hambre común, de sufrimientos comunes, no le habían
> bastado para conocer a su esposa. Sintió que algo había
> envejecido en el amor. (49)

For forty years they have been sharing suffering, and in that
time the Colonel has failed to notice changes in their
relationship, just as 'Su esposa lo vio en ese instante, vestido

como el día de su matrimonio. Sólo entonces advirtió cuánto
había envejecido su esposo' (6). Despite his wife's outward
resilience, summed up by her courageous recoveries and by the
way even her questions sound positive ('Los trastornos
respiratorios la obligaban a preguntar afirmando', 4), she has
feelings that he cannot fathom. But when the Colonel recognises
the effect of suffering on her, he is afraid to let her express her
grief:

> En el curso del almuerzo el coronel comprendió que su
> esposa se estaba forzando para no llorar. Esa certidumbre
> lo alarmó. Conocía el carácter de su mujer, naturalmente
> duro, y endurecido todavía más por cuarenta años de
> amargura. La muerte de su hijo no le arrancó una lágrima.
> Fijó directamente en sus ojos una mirada de
> reprobación. Ella se mordió los labios, se secó los
> párpados con la manga y siguió almorzando. (69-70)

He is alarmed by her almost crying because it is not what he is
used to; if she weakens, so will he. He needs her strength if not
her understanding.

Although the majority of the population of 'el pueblo' suffers
in some way, usually as a result of the political situation of the
time, the most acute suffering is reserved throughout for the
Colonel and his wife. As Vargas Llosa points out, the meaning
of poverty for them is that their house is mortgaged and will
probably be taken away in two years (34), they live on credit
and, which worries the Colonel more, lies. They have to eat the
cock's maize (46), his wife makes stone soup because she is
ashamed to let their neighbours see their want (50). While
politics is the basis of the social chronicle of the novel, hunger
and misery is the basis of the individual biography (*33*, p.314).

Although poorer than the other members of the community
(for example, Don Sabas's serfs are paid, the apprentices have
money for gambling), the Colonel is treated with respect by the
doctor, by Germán in the cockpit, even by Don Sabas (compare
1, p.x with *33*, p.114). But respect, although a bolster to his
pride, does not remove the shame of having to beg, and it does

not regain lost influence. Influence in the town is now in the hands of three people: Don Sabas, the mayor and Padre Ángel.

Don Sabas is the only other character, after the Colonel and his wife, about whom conflicting opinions are expressed. With his first appearance in the novel, he is presented in contrast to the Colonel:

> Era don Sabas, el padrino de su hijo muerto, el único dirigente de su partido que escapó a la persecución política y continuaba viviendo en el pueblo...
> Don Sabas carraspeó. Sostenía el paraguas con la mano izquierda, el mango casi a la altura de la cabeza pues era más bajo que el coronel. (9)

Pontiero says:

> This special relationship between the dead Agustín and Don Sabas as his godfather helps to explain why the colonel continues to befriend the old miser whose political treachery and corrupt methods of self-enrichment are common knowledge. The fact that Don Sabas has not been brought to justice also suggests that unholy alliances and secret pacts continue to operate in the town. (*1*, Endnote E, p.75)

Don Sabas's treachery is not clearly stated until the doctor calls the Colonel ingenuous for believing anything honourable about him (59). When he offers four hundred rather than nine hundred pesos for the cock he shows that he is unscrupulous, and the reason he gives is callous in view of Agustín's death: 'Pero ahora nadie se atreve a soltar un buen gallo. Siempre hay el riesgo de salir muerto a tiros de la gallera' (58). His lack of principle is opposite to the Colonel's strength of character, just as his new, two-storey house (11) and his obesity and diabetes (43, 57) contrast with the Colonel's poor dwelling and malnutrition. In his position of influence through ill-gotten wealth, Don Sabas has no need to be aware of the state of siege (10) while the Colonel has every reason to remember, since his son was shot as a result of it.

By his words and actions, Don Sabas shows that differing opinions about him are not justified. Similarly, his wife, who prattles on to the Colonel, mainly about death (44, 53), and who bickers with her husband, is a contrast with the Colonel's wife. But her physique ('Era corpulenta, más alta que su marido, y con una verruga pilosa en el labio superior', 44) and her hypochondria ('El médico quedó en la sala requerido por la mujer de don Sabas que le pidió un remedio "para esas cosas que de pronto le dan a uno y que no se sabe qué es"', 58) show her to be greedy and weak. Compared with the Colonel and his wife's marriage, that of Don Sabas and his wife, says Pontiero, 'borders on caricature...Don Sabas and his wife torment each other with their foolish fears and suspicions, lost to the world and each other amidst the confusion of their hoarded possessions' (*1*, p.xviii).

The mayor appears briefly:

> Vio al alcalde en el balcón del cuartel en una actitud discursiva. Estaba en calzoncillos y franela, hinchada la mejilla sin afeitar. Los músicos suspendieron la marcha fúnebre. Un momento después el coronel reconoció la voz del padre Ángel conversando a gritos con el alcalde. (9-10)

His corrupt deal with Don Sabas (59) does not secure his position because he is petrified that a poor musician's funeral may become an insurrection. He belongs to the class of people described by Pontiero as:

> neurotic and grotesque...To offset their worldly wealth and power they are plagued by every manner of strange ailment and disorder. They go in fear and mistrust of everyone and succumb with alarming regularity to that enigmatic malady — *rabia*, so that, far from exciting the envy of the poor, they attract ridicule and even compassion. (*1*, p.xix)

One must disagree with Pontiero here because, firstly, 'rabia' is not once mentioned in the text; second, Don Sabas's emotions are not enigmatic: he is transparently mean, bad-tempered and self-centred. His ailments are not strange, being the result of over-eating. His wife's hypochondria, although psychosomatic, is not unusal either, nor is the mayor's swollen cheek.

Pontiero underlines the religious undertones of García Márquez's portrayal of rich and poor by quoting Luke 18.18, 'It is easier for a camel to pass through the eye of a needle than for a rich man to enter into the Kingdom of God' and, as a contrast, Matthew 5.3, 'Blessed are the poor in spirit: for theirs is the Kingdom of Heaven' (*1*, pp.xviii-xix). Certainly, the rich are presented as having little hope of redemption, but the poor are not necessarily poor in spirit. The Colonel is ultimately shown as having strength of spirit and even though his wife does not share his resolve to face a bleak future, her ability to overcome her asthma displays determination. One can agree that 'García Márquez makes no attempt to disguise the injustice or humiliation of poverty...Yet that poverty also seems to ennoble the lives of the colonel and his wife', but they are not 'socially unacceptable and ostracised' (*1*, p.xviii). Perhaps, of the Beatitudes in Matthew 5, verse 6 is as relevant to the Colonel, if not more so, as verse 3: 'Blessed are they which do hunger and thirst after righteousness: for they shall be filled.'

Padre Ángel imposes moral censorship on films by ringing the church bells, then sits outside the cinema taking the names of those who disobey him (48). That he shows no respect for his calling by being prepared to repress and spy on people gives little weight to his telling the Colonel's wife 'Que es pecado negociar con las cosas sagradas' (49). The priest and the mayor also appear in *La mala hora* (and the latter with his swollen cheek in 'Un día de éstos'), and in discussing their character Pontiero seems to include elements from outside *El coronel* (*1*, pp.xx-xxi). The mayor's fears of losing office are only loosely implied in the text, while neither the priest's age nor his memories of youthful aspirations are mentioned. Vargas Llosa also provides extratextual information on members of 'el pueblo': he calls Don Sabas's serfs 'guajiros', that is Indians from the Guajira Peninsula, but nowhere in the text are they referred to as such

(*33*, pp.300-04; in *La hojarasca*, peasants are called 'guajiros').

The peasants are on the bottom level of the town's strata of society. Above them is the foreman, who relays Don Sabas's orders and pay (52-53). There are two passing references to Indians: the most important is that the policeman who threatens the Colonel and who shot Agustín is 'aindiado' (61). The other reference is:'Nada sacamos con que nos la metan en el cajón como a los indios' (27). In each case there is a sense of disapproval towards the Indians. The Indian policeman belongs to the forces of repression; in the second case, the suggestion is that, normally, the Indians are poorer than the people of the Colonel and his wife's class, especially to the Colonel's wife's mind. (Because the musician is buried with his trumpet, there is no suggestion that this custom is heathen; see *1*, Endnote 0, p.76, and *33*, p.294.)

Within what Vargas Llosa calls the 'clase media' come the German watch-repairer (39) and the Syrian shopkeepers at the quayside (*33*, p.300). Moisés, the Syrian with whom the Colonel comes into direct contact (64), is in an intermediate position in the town. As Pontiero points out, he has lived in 'el pueblo' long enough almost to forget his native tongue, yet, as the Colonel's wife's confession, 'Estuve hasta donde los turcos' (49), shows, having dealings with him and his fellow merchants inspires distrust and humiliation (*1*, p.xxii). But when Moisés says that circus tightrope-walkers eat cats to prevent their bones breaking (64), he too is showing distrust of outsiders (*1*, Endnote W, p.78). What Pontiero omits to say is that the Colonel, in paying more attention to the circus or to the postal administrator, is uncharacteristically humourless towards Moisés. The Syrian says that he would be 897 years old if the weather was always good, but the Colonel replies that he would be his proper age, seventy-five. One can also include in the town's middle class the officials such as the postal administrator, and the people who pass through (the circus folk, the black charlatan, 66).

Between the middle and professional classes are the tailor's apprentices, Germán, Álvaro and Alfonso, of whom Pontiero says: 'Their contact with the colonel is limited to clandestine meetings and hasty exchanges of subversive propaganda' (*1*, p.xxii). True, they do provide the Colonel with clandestine information, which Blanco Aguinaga says shows signs of their overcoming oppression (*9*, p.57), but their meetings are not secret: in the tailor's shop (38-41), in the billiard hall (61), in the cockpit (65); and, although not directly shown, they go to his house to tend the cock.

The two representatives of the professional class are the doctor and the lawyer. The doctor, like the apprentices, is part of the subversive movement, but we never see him contact them, only the Colonel. He has no illusions about the political situation:

—No hay esperanzas de elecciones—dijo el coronel.
—No sea ingenuo, coronel—dijo el médico—. Ya nosotros estamos muy grandes para esperar al Mesías. (15)

Nor has he any illusions about the corruption of others. But he is also humorous when speaking to the Colonel's wife (18-19, 35) and with the Colonel at Don Sabas's expense (56-57).

Just as the doctor has no illusions, so the lawyer has none about the impossible task he has in dealing with bureaucracy. After the Colonel has told him that his services are no longer required, the lawyer says:

'Como usted diga, coronel', dijo, espantando los animales. 'Será como usted diga. Si yo pudiera hacer milagros no estaría viviendo en este corral.' (29-30)

He is a representative of a profession that is a target for social satire (see *1*, pp.xxi-xxii, and *22*, p.169, on attacks on lawyers in *Cien años de soledad*). But here the attack goes beyond the lawyer himself, aiming at the system that can breed such an ineffective man who lives in chaos and relies on hackneyed expressions ('La unión hace la fuerza', 28). The physical description of him is pathetic:

Era un negro monumental sin nada más que los dos

colmillos en la mandíbula superior...Estaba aplastado por el calor. Forzó hacia atrás los resortes de la silla y se abanicó con un cartón de propaganda...La silla era demasiado estrecha para sus nalgas otoñales. (27-28)

His unsuitability for his profession is summed up in these few lines, and is in direct contrast to the doctor, who 'Era un médico joven con el cráneo cubierto de rizos charolados. Había algo increíble en la perfección de su sistema dental' (14). He conforms to the medical stereotype of having illegible handwriting, but it is his teeth that have 'el estereotipado esmalte' (19). His perfect teeth, mentioned again on page 57 and in *La mala hora* ('Vio reflejada en el agua su propia reacción: un sistema dental tan correcto que no parecía natural', *4*, p.102), exemplify García Márquez's technique of describing characters with a few evocative details, to be discussed more fully in Chapter 5 below.

The interaction between the major and minor characters encompasses both the political and social themes. On the fundamental level, all live in a poor, isolated town under state of siege, but the reason that the town is this way is that those in political authority institutionalize repression and are too busy lining their own pockets. Don Sabas calls it a 'pueblo de mierda' (42), but he is one of the few people who could do something to change it (by spending money to improve it). The way that political and social elements are interwoven is demonstrated by the everyday meetings between the Colonel, his wife and other people. Almost every contact is related to their dire straits. The Colonel meets the doctor at the post wharf when waiting for a letter (which will bring money to ease his suffering, but which does not arrive because of stifling bureaucracy). The doctor exchanges political information with him, as do the apprentices. He meets them before and after going to the post, and over the sale of the clock. He meets Moisés on his way to the post wharf, the lawyer to dismiss him in order to speed things up, and Don Sabas over the sale of the cock. At the musician's funeral, the Colonel's contact with Don Sabas and other people (the musician's mother, for example), has direct relevance to the political theme. When the Colonel confronts Germán in the cockpit, both themes are present: the cock is a legacy of the dead Agustín, and therefore has political connotations, while its fight and possible victory have social overtones in that the Colonel and others may gain financially.

Most contact is with the Colonel. His wife meets the doctor with the Colonel, to be treated for her ill-health. She also meets Padre Ángel to try to pawn the wedding rings. There is no political element, only social, in her meetings because, as Castagnino says, she moves outside her husband's circle (*11*, p.96).

When people meet, there is the additional level of communication, through speech or visual contact. Speech, in the form of directness, argument, lies or humour, or lack of speech, reveal emotional traits. Doris Rolfe, as will be shown in Chapter 5, argues that the most telling emotions are neither spoken nor shown, but there are many occasions when people together act 'en silencio'. The Colonel and his wife contemplate the cock in silence (5); Don Sabas and the Colonel walk beside each other in silence (9); women watch the funeral cortège in silence, biting their nails (10); the doctor and the Colonel return from the dock in silence (15); the doctor responds silently to the Colonel's wife (19); and there are a number of references to silence between the Colonel and his wife in the final chapter. Silence signifies a lack of, or a lack of a need for, communication; on many occasions eye contact is more revealing than speech.

Y entonces vio de cerca, por la primera vez en su vida, al hombre que disparó contra su hijo. Estaba exactamente frente a él con el cañón del fusil apuntando contra su vientre. Era pequeño, aindiado, de piel curtida, y exhalaba un tufo infantil. El coronel apretó los dientes y apartó suavemente con la punta de los dedos el cañón del fusil.

—Permiso—dijo.

Se enfrentó a unos pequeños y redondos ojos de murciélago. En un instante se sintió tragado por esos ojos, triturado, digerido e inmediatamente expulsado.

—Pase usted, coronel. (61)

> Entonces saltó la barrera, se abrió paso a través de la
> multitud concentrada en el redondel y se enfrentó a los
> tranquilos ojos de Germán. Se miraron sin parpadear.
> —Buenas tardes, coronel.
> El coronel le quitó el gallo. 'Buenas tardes', murmuró.
> Y no dijo nada más porque lo estremeció la caliente y
> profunda palpitación del animal. (65-66)

In each of these confrontations, hardly a word is said, but words
are superfluous. Similarly:

> El administrador buscó en las casillas clasificadas.
> Cuando acabó de leer repuso las cartas en la letra
> correspondiente pero no dijo nada. Se sacudió la palma de
> las manos y dirigió al coronel una mirada significativa.
> (46)

This can be compared with the time that the postman actually
says 'Nada para el coronel' (14), but does not look at him,
emphasizing the ritual of repeating that there are no letters.

How people use their eyes, or how eyes meet, underlines the
way in which characters respond inscrutably to being watched:
political strife has bred a suspicious society (see *1*, pp.xxv-xxvi).
Padre Ángel, when checking on those going to the cinema
'vigilaba', a word with connotations of thoroughness and prying
(48). Don Sabas's eyes, sad like a toad's (42) and colourless (56),
have a completely empty gaze, but they inspire pity in the
Colonel (45). On seeing the Colonel, Don Sabas 'no reveló
ninguna reacción' (53). The doctor examines the Colonel 'con
una mirada absolutamente desprovista de interés profesional'
(59), but his 'hermetismo insólito' (59) makes it hard to tell if he
is uninterested, or if his unprofessional look is one of comradely
concern. Germán has penetrating green eyes, which he fixes on
the Colonel (39, 41). 'Germán fue quien comprendió' (41); he
realized the Colonel's plight without having to be told what the
problem was. Alfonso wears glasses (40), Álvaro's eyes are
'alucinados' (38), but the Colonel feels surrounded by 'rostros
herméticos' when in the apprentices' company (39).

Many characteristics of the visual communication of the Colonel and his wife, as with so many other aspects of the novel, appear in the first chapter.

—Mira en lo que ha quedado nuestro paraguas de payaso de circo—dijo el coronel con una antigua frase suya. Abrió sobre su cabeza un misterioso sistema de varillas metálicas—. Ahora sólo sirve para contar las estrellas.

Sonrió. Pero la mujer no se tomó el trabajo de mirar el paraguas. 'Todo está así', murmuró. 'Nos estamos pudriendo vivos.' Y cerró los ojos para pensar más intensamente en el muerto.

Después de afeitarse al tacto—pues carecía de espejo desde hacía mucho tiempo—el coronel se vistió en silencio...Su esposa lo vio en este instante, vestido como el día de su matrimonio. Sólo entonces advirtió cuánto había envejecido su esposo...

Él trató de doblegar con un peine de cuerno las cerdas color de acero. Pero fue un esfuerzo inútil.

—Debo parecer un papagayo—dijo.

La mujer lo examinó. Pensó que no. El coronel no parecía un papagayo. Era un hombre árido, de huesos sólidos articulados a tuerca y tornillo. Por la vitalidad de sus ojos no parecía conservado en formol. (6-7)

The Colonel's humorous but well-worn phrase about the clown's umbrella is an example of the fact that 'In the colonel's eyes, the world, for all its nastiness, remains full of surprising possibilities' (*1*, p.xii). His ability to inject harsh reality with a sense of fun and mystery is not shared by his wife who does not take the trouble to look at the umbrella. She regards it as a symbol of rot and closes her eyes to his vision of life to return to her fixation on death. When she does open her eyes, she sees her husband as he was and as he is now, and again, she does not join with his humour: he is not like a parrot.

The Colonel's eyes are full of life, and their appearance is that of syrup, exactly same as his wife's. Their eyes meet during a discussion about how to feed themselves and the cock, and his wife accedes to his priority of buying maize for the bird, rather than coffee and cheese for themselves (22). A second direct contact occurs during one of the wife's asthmatic attacks, brought about by a verbal outburst on the cock and its causing Agustín's death:

> Sus ojos tropezaron con otros ojos exactamente iguales a los suyos. 'Trata de no moverte', dijo, sintiendo los silbidos dentro de sus propios pulmones. La mujer cayó en un sopor momentáneo. Cerró los ojos. Cuando volvió a abrirlos su respiración parecía más reposada. (37)

She feels better after closing her eyes on the reality that contains the cock. Finally, the Colonel 'Fijó directamente en sus ojos una mirada de reprobación' (70). Although he does not have to tell his wife not to show weakness, his look brings on a verbal attack against him: 'Eres un desconsiderado'. In these three exchanges, the meeting of their eyes shows the progression of bitter emotions that the Colonel's wife feels towards her husband and his attitude to the cock.

During the closing hours of the story, the Colonel either replies stubbornly or remains silent to his wife's complaints and accusations. At one moment, he wants to forget everything, sleep through to January, 'Pero se sabía amenazado por la vigilia de la mujer' (71). He tells her to go to sleep, while he:

> Trató de tener los ojos abiertos, pero lo quebrantó el sueño. Cayó hasta el fondo de una substancia sin tiempo y sin espacio, donde las palabras de su mujer tenían un significado diferente. Pero un instante después se sintió sacudido por el hombro.
> —Contéstame.
> El coronel no supo si había oído esa palabra antes o después del sueño...Le ardían los ojos y tuvo que hacer un gran esfuerzo para recobrar la lucidez. (72)

His wife wakes him to face a reality in which, thanks to his decision to keep the cock, he is alone (despite his protestations to the contrary), and the only sustenance is excrement. But he is unable to explain himself to his wife, causing this final series of uncomprehending exchanges, punctuated by darkness and light, and lacking in proper visual and verbal communication. On an earlier occasion, when no letter came for him:

> Habría preferido permanecer allí hasta el viernes siguiente para no presentarse esa noche ante su mujer con las manos vacías. Pero cuando cerraron la sastrería tuvo que hacerle frente a la realidad. (26)

Now, though, he is fully aware of, and unrepentant about, the reality that he has chosen to accept: 'Al primer canto del gallo tropezó con la realidad, pero volvió a hundirse en un sueño denso, seguro, sin remordimientos' (69).

4 *Symbols and Imagery*

In this chapter, symbols and images will be studied together because the compactness and inner tensions of *El coronel* are indicated, among other ways, by the interlinking of symbols (objects which also stand for something else) and images (in both the figurative and the representational sense).

There are three principal symbols in the novel. Without doubt, that which is accorded most importance by critics is the fighting cock, but there is less agreement about whether the dead son Agustín or the letter should accompany it in a position of dominance. All three are, to borrow Pontiero's term, silent. The cock is present but unable to communicate for biological reasons, although:

> El gallo produjo un sonido gutural que llegó hasta el corredor como una sorda conversación humana. 'A veces pienso que ese animal va a hablar', dijo la mujer. (47)

Agustín, having been killed, is unable to communicate with his parents, except in their memory (for example, 37). The long-awaited letter is bureaucratic silence. It could be argued that the absent objects are merely a dead character and a non-existent piece of paper and as such should not be regarded as true symbols, but each has deep significance for the protagonists and is inextricably bound up with their predicament. Furthermore, the recurrence of each in the text, tied to its relation to the other and to the cock, invests it with more potency than that of an image.

Castagnino, in his discussion of the signs that are transformed into symbols in *El coronel*, turns his attention to the cock and the letter (*11*, p.130).[17] The cock, he says, means in the story a

[17] On signs, Castagnino says:
Toda obra literaria es sistema de signos que contiene otros varios sistemas con códigos propios...
La relación semántica concierne a los significados de los signos. Todo

fighting animal upon which one bets; it denotes (indicates) that its triumph will bring about its owner's financial recuperation. On the symbolic level, it represents barbarity and primitive culture and connotes (implies) the memory of the killed son; the character of the symbol is positive and it functions as a symbol of hope. Critics who have not adopted this formal approach to the text give a number of connotations to the bird. More important than the various interpretations is the fact that, for the characters, the cock symbolises different things. This has been pointed out by Vargas Llosa (*33*, p.316) and Rowe (*32*), and is not adequately covered by Castagnino.

Cockfighting is a popular sport throughout Colombia and García Márquez uses the fighting cock as a motif of his native land (*33*, p.48). But unlike the glorification of the sport in some Latin American fiction, in *El coronel* the cockpit represents provincial sordidness and daily horror (*34*, p.167). In the novel, the barbarity is emphasised by the immense monetary value attached to a bird which is bred to kill (or be killed) and by the shooting, without trial, of political opponents in the cockpit. Even for the dead, the sport's popularity is great:

...la mujer seguía pensando en el muerto.
—Ya debe haberse encontrado con Agustín—dijo—.
Pueda ser que no le cuente la situación en que quedamos
después de su muerte.
—A esta hora estarán discutiendo de gallos—dijo el
coronel. (5)

The implication is that Agustín would not even care about his parents' suffering, so keen was he on cockfighting.

The value of the cock changes throughout the story. Initially it 'Vale como cincuenta pesos...Ya se sabe con seguridad que hay peleas en enero. Después podemos venderlo a mejor precio' (12). It is a link between the past (their son) and the future. The Colonel sees it as his duty to his son to keep the cock, put it in

signo designa su significado y anuncia su significación. Por aquél, nombra; por ésta, denota. Pero, además puede remitir a una referencialidad, por un mecanismo evocativo: es su connotación. (*11*, pp.124-26) the pit and obtain a good price for it (36). When the Colonel considers selling the cock before the fight its price leaps to 900 pesos, 'la cifra más alta que el coronel había tenido en su cabeza después de que restituyó los fondos de la revolución' (45), declining to 400 pesos with Don Sabas's circumspection (58). The value given to it by Agustín's companions, according to the Colonel's first impressions, concerns money: '—Entusiasmados—informó el coronel—. Todos están ahorrando para apostarle al gallo' (12); 'Lo que me preocupa es que esos pobres muchachos están ahorrando' (21); also breeding: 'Trajeron una gallina vieja para enrazarla con el gallo' (47). This inspires the Colonel to recall Colonel Aureliano Buendía, another link with his revolutionary past. To begin with, the Colonel's wife sees it as a bird of no worth ('No sé qué le han visto a ese gallo tan feo', 12), and while it is only worth fifty pesos she tells the Colonel to give it to the apprentices (36). When its value has gone up and it is 'un gallo contante y sonante...Nos dará para comer tres años' (47), she does not immediately tell her husband to sell it, but soon does (54). From being, for her, the source of their son's death (37), it becomes a real answer to her misery. To her mind, it cannot be got rid of quickly enough: 'No veo la hora de salir de este pájaro de mal agüero' (62).

Unfortunately, the old woman is unable to make her husband stick to his decision to sell the cock because at the cock-fight trials he realises that the cock means more than just money or a duty to his son. When he picks up the bird, 'Pensó que nunca había tenido una cosa tan viva entre las manos' (66). He also hears the spectators' rapturous reception which revives political memories and, allied to the life of the cock, new sensibilities. His change of heart is shown:

—Dijeron que se lo llevarían por encima de nuestros cadáveres—dijo—. Dijeron que el gallo no era nuestro sino de todo el pueblo.
Sólo cuando terminó con el gallo el coronel se enfrentó al rostro trastornado de su mujer. Descubrió sin asombro que no le producía remordimiento ni compasión.

'Hicieron bien', dijo calmadamente. Y luego, registrándose los bolsillos, agregó con una especie de insondable dulzura:

—El gallo no se vende. (67)

And later,

—Si el doctor me garantiza que vendiendo el gallo se te quita el asma, lo vendo en seguida—dijo—. Pero si no, no. (70)

Remorselessness and lack of compassion do not remove all his sympathies, but the value of the cock for him now transcends physical suffering and mourning their dead son. It is something tangible on which to pin his hopes (*17*, p.327).

Rowe sees the Colonel's reaction to the trials as the turning point when he decides not to sell the bird (*32*). Rolfe also points to the importance of this passage (*31*, pp.346-47). When the cock finally takes the place of the long-awaited letter, the Colonel's dilemma changes. First it is an interior struggle, described by Pontiero as follows:

If he should part with the bird he would be betraying the dead Agustín and his future hopes of eliminating all his debts, yet should he go on refusing to sell it for some ready cash the chances are that the cock will lose the contest and that he and his wife will die from starvation. (*1*, p.xxix)

It becomes exteriorised when he realises that if he sells the bird he will be betraying the people; the alternative, hunger, remains the same. Because there are strong political links between the cock and the characters, Rolfe and Rama see the cock as a symbol of political resistance (*31*, p.346; *29*, pp.67-68). García Márquez himself implies that it is not a symbol of the repressed forces of the people, stressing instead the face value of the book.[18] This is not as much an oversimplification as it may

[18] 'La Poésie à la portée de tous', *Magazine Littéraire* (Paris), no. 178 (1981), p.31.

appear because it is Agustín, whose name is used as a code for
clandestine information (39, 60), who symbolises resistance for
those opposed to authority. The cock, as a legacy of Agustín, is
a 'symbol of collective hope' (*1*, p.xxix): as well as the vulgar
possibility of winning money, the hope that Agustín did not die
in vain. This point is echoed by Earle:

> El gallo, en esta obra, representa la resurrección de un
> pueblo sujeto a varias formas de opresión: la censura
> política y religiosa, el estado de sitio impuesto por el
> gobierno central, la injusticia concretada en la mala
> economía, el asesinato como castigo.[19]

Vargas Llosa argues that the political significance of the cock
lies in its relationship with chance; it is important that the most
adamant terrorists are the most enthusiastic players of roulette
and gamblers in the cockpit (*33*, pp.318-20). While they will do
their best to ensure the cock's victory (by feeding it, taking it by
force from the Colonel's house to the trials), their irrational
faith in its success must eventually be matched by the equally
confident owners of another cock. In the same way, their hopes
that their subversive activities will be successful have always to
face the powers-that-be (who killed Agustín in the cockpit, and
who raid the roulette game in the billiard hall).

The cockfight trials are a key episode in the development of
the cock's value; they also act as a culmination to its physical
presentation. It is first described by the Colonel's wife: 'tiene la
cabeza muy chiquita para las patas' (12; there is a misprint here
in *1*, 'la patas' for 'las patas'). It is described later, impersonally:
'Estaba listo para los entrenamientos. El cuello y los muslos
pelados y cárdenos, la cresta rebanada, el animal había
adquirido una figura escueta, un aire indefenso' (62). In the

---

[19] Peter G. Earle, 'El futuro como espejismo' in *Gabriel García Márquez*, pp.81-
90, at p.86. In a footnote, Earle notes that Sir James G. Frazer relates the cock
with primitive European harvest rituals, especially as in maize spirits. Thus, says
Earle, the bird for the primitive peoples, and in *El coronel*, was 'un arma
simbólica contra el hambre' (p.86). Earle refers to *The Golden Bough*, One-
volume Abridged Edition (New York: Macmillan, 1963), pp.522-24. In the
London: Macmillan, 1957 edition, the reference is to pp.592-94.

intervening period, factual comments about its health in preparation for the fighting ('el gallo está emplumando', 41; the talk of its injection, 44-45), contrast with the personification of the bird:

> El gallo estaba perfectamente vivo frente al tarro vacío. Cuando vio al coronel emitió un monólogo gutural, casi humano, y echó la cabeza hacia atras. Él le hizo una sonrisa de complicidad:
> —La vida es dura, camarada. (37)

> El gallo produjo un sonido gutural que llegó hasta el corredor como una sorda conversación humana. 'A veces pienso que ese animal va a hablar', dijo la mujer. (47)

Added to this almost human quality is the idea that it feeds off its owners: 'Cuando se acabe el maíz tendremos que alimentarlo con nuestros hígados' (12); 'Ese animal se alimenta de carne humana' (59). This is inverted when the maize brought for the cock feeds the Colonel and his wife (46), after which it seems a different bird to its owner (47). Bollettino says of the personification of the bird:

> El gallo se impone en la vida de los protagonistas hasta convertirse en el personaje principal con capacidad de determinar el destino de todos los habitantes del pueblo. Ellos se animalizarán mientras el gallo seguirá adquiriendo características humanas a medida que su importancia crece. (*10*, p.55)

The preparations and the personification end in the cockpit. After the Colonel sees his bird 'en el centro de la pista, solo, indefenso, las espuelas envueltas en trapos, con algo de miedo evidente en el temblor de las patas', the confrontation between the two cocks is presented bluntly, 'Fue una sucesión de asaltos iguales. Una instantánea trabazón de plumas y patas y pescuezos en el centro de una alborotada ovación...Pero ahora sus patas no temblaban' (65). Even though the cock is now fulfilling the purpose for which it has been bred, to the Colonel 'Le pareció una farsa a la cual—voluntaria y conscientemente—se prestaban también los gallos' (65). In contrast to the tragedy of the Colonel's situation, it is a farcical spectacle from which the Colonel momentarily stands apart, registering 'la desproporción entre el entusiasmo de la ovación y la intensidad del espectáculo'. That both men and cocks lend themselves to the theatre underlines, in Rowe's words, 'the idea that meanings are made by men and depend on them' (*32*).

The strong links between the cock and its previous owner, Agustín, have already been mentioned. Vargas Llosa says that Agustín's killing is only told in relation to the cock (*33*, p.308). As well as the reference to his death on page 12, there is the Colonel's wife's description of the event (37). Pontiero says she is bitter, but, overcome by shock and grief, she did not shed a tear at the death of her son (*1*, p.xxvii; see 70). There is just as strong a suggestion that it is her toughness that prevents her from showing grief. The loss of her son is included in her bitterness at the misery caused by unfulfilled promises:

> La mujer abandonó el mosquitero y se dirigió a la hamaca. 'Estoy dispuesta a acabar con los remilgos y las contemplaciones en esta casa', dijo. Su voz empezó a oscurecerse de cólera. 'Estoy hasta la coronilla de resignación y dignidad.'
> El coronel no movió un músculo.
> —Veinte años esperando los pajaritos de colores que te prometieron después de cada elección y de todo eso nos queda un hijo muerto—prosiguió ella—. Nada más que un hijo muerto. (50)

As far as she is concerned, the death of her son goes no further than the futility of the individual trying to overcome the system. She does not share her husband's desire to keep alive Agustín's aspirations for the cock, nor does she share the townsfolk's regard for him as a symbol of continued opposition even after his demise.

Her bitter remark 'Nosotros somos huérfanos de nuestro hijo' (13) has two strata of meaning: first, although he worked all his life (as his father says, 30), he left them only a sewing machine, the proceeds of which are just about exhaused (21), and a cock, which is eating his parents alive. The second level is the implication that Agustín and his bird were the representatives of the family that the town held in highest esteem. Despite the Colonel's past, it is only the survival of the cock which accords the father and mother any respect. As a symbol, Agustín is positive for the town, providing hope, but negative for his despairing mother.

Whereas the links between the cock and Agustín operate on the political level, those between the cock and the letter refer to the social and political themes. Castagnino's description of the letter is as follows: it is a communication that is awaited, it denotes delay, a breakdown in the system; it represents bureaucracy and implies inaction; unlike the cock it is negative in character, but also inspires hope (*11*, p.130). This only gives the political level, and fails to take into account the content of the letter. If and when it comes, it will provide a pension, that is to say money to relieve the misery of the Colonel and his wife. The indication of breakdown of the system leads to the political implications, while the delay leads to the social implications.

The social level is indicated by the precariousness of the mail launch's journey compared to aeroplane travel; lack of communication is made worse by isolation (24). It can also be found in conjunction with the Colonel's ill-health:

> También el coronel sufrió una recaída. Agonizó muchas horas en el excusado, sudando hielo, sintiendo que se pudría y se caía a pedazos la flora de sus vísceras. 'Es el invierno', se repitió sin desesperarse. 'Todo será distinto cuando acabe de llover.' Y lo creyó realmente, seguro de estar vivo en el momento en que llegara la carta. (35)

In the Colonel's mind, the letter and money are inseparable: after Don Sabas tells him that the cock is worth 900 pesos, the Colonel says to the postal administrator: '—Estoy esperando una carta urgente—dijo—. Es por avion...Tenía que llegarme hoy con seguridad' (46). From the firm expectation of a letter at this point, the Colonel's hopes decline sharply, to be replaced by trust in the cock's victory. Although the awaited letter's importance as a cause of the Colonel's condition may fade, its role as a symbol of bureaucratic failure does not because nothing changes in the novel to show an improvement in the state of affairs. It is worth noting, as does Jitrik, that 'en lugar de la carta esperada públicamente viene el folleto que hay que guardar en silencio y en el cual, presumiblemente, están las razones que podrían explicar por qué no llega la carta'.[20]

Something in the novel that is seen to change is the weather. The heat and the rain of October are an inescapable fact: 'Octubre era una de las pocas cosas que llegaban' (3), but the thought of better weather inspires optimism, even in November which is worse than October (35). The weather is not strictly a metaphor for the Colonel's state of mind, because he feels that the heat and humidity cause unnatural growths in his stomach and the combined external and internal pressures contribute to the weakening of his resolve. Unlike his frustration, though, the constipation disappears when the weather brightens: 'Diciembre había marchitado la flora de sus vísceras' (63). He not only becomes more cheerful, but he regains his resilience. The fine morning of the cockfight trials transforms his house and prefigures his subsequent clarity of purpose:

Era un patio maravilloso, con la hierba y los árboles y el cuartito del excusado flotando en la claridad, a un milímetro sobre el nivel del suelo. (62)

Salió a la calle estimulado por el presentimiento de que esa tarde llegaría la carta. Como aún no era la hora de las lanchas esperó a don Sabas en su oficina. Pero le confirmaron que no llegaría sino el lunes. No se desesperó a pesar de que no había previsto ese contratiempo. 'Tarde o temprano tiene que venir', se dijo, y se dirigió al puerto, en un instante prodigioso, hecho de una claridad todavía

[20] 'Las frases productoras en *El coronel no tiene quien le escriba*', in Gabriel García Márquez, *El coronel no tiene quien le escriba. La increíble y triste historia de la cándida Eréndira y de su abuela desalmada*. Selección y estudio preliminar por Noé Jitrik (Buenos Aires: Librería del Colegio, 1976), pp.17-24, at pp.22-23.

sin usar. (63)

At one point, García Márquez prevents the weather being a metaphor for the wife's temper:

> Su voz empezó a oscurecerse de cólera...
> La interrumpió el relámpago. El trueno se despedazó en la calle, entró al dormitorio y pasó rodando por debajo de la cama como un tropel de piedras. La mujer saltó hacia el mosquitero en busca del rosario.
> El coronel sonrió.
> —Esto te pasa por no frenar la lengua. (50-51)

The stereotyped image of anger like a storm (or vice versa) is broken when the Colonel quips that the storm is a punishment for his wife's chiding too much.

Ernesto Volkening says that tropical weather reflects the state of mind of tropical man: omnipresent heat represents monotony, it fills the space around the characters, acting as a unifying medium. He says, 'el arte narrativo de García Márquez se alimenta de una obsesión meteorológico-barométrico' (*36*, pp.79-80). Blanco Aguinaga declares that the October weather is symbolic:

> El hecho de que cuando conocemos al Coronel llueva lenta y largamente (aparte de que es la temporada de lluvias) viene a subrayar de manera simbólica el estancamiento de la Historia, su aparente falta de futuro, al igual que refuerzan simbólicamente la idea del lejano origen de la opresión el entierro al que se dirige el Coronel cuando le vemos por primera vez, y la no-carta que hace quince años que no llega para anunciarle la esperada nueva de la pensión merecida desde hace cincuenta. (*9*, p.57)

Rain, he says, is a natural Colombian symbol to show oppression and immobility. It is true that no one is exempt from the effects of the weather or of political repression, but it does not rain all year. The rain as a symbol of oppression, like the metaphor of the Colonel's constipation, acts figuratively within the text because the arrival of better weather resolves nothing.

The presentation of the weather is woven into a net of images. 'La llovizna le maltrató los párpados' (9): the violence of this phrase recalls the political violence of the times and the basic violence of cockfighting. The Colonel's past profession is echoed in military imagery used with the weather: 'Pero octubre concedió una tregua el viernes en la tarde' (12), 'Octubre prolongó la tregua' (23), 'El trueno se despedazó en la calle, entró al dormitorio y pasó rodando por debajo de la cama como un tropel de piedras' (50). The phrases, 'las minúsculas tiendas de las lombrices en el barro' (4), and 'acosado por los zancudos' (16), have both military and meteorological overtones (worm casts and mosquitoes are usually associated with wet weather). Military imagery without climatic associations is repeated when the Colonel and his wife are talking: '—No importa que esté la tropa en su oficina...—Van a creer que estamos preparando un asalto', and in the doctor's joke '—Habrá que fusilarlo' (56); also 'Uno de los niños amenazó al coronel con una escopeta de palo' (48) and 'se sintió con fuerzas para avanzar' (41). In the final paragraph of the novel 'invencible' has military connotations, as does 'vigilar' (36, 48).

Metallic imagery has already been mentioned in relation to the Colonel's hair and joints (see p.32 above), but it recurs with reference to the weather:

> Él encendió la lámpara para localizar la gotera en la sala. Puso debajo el tarro del gallo y regresó al dormitorio perseguido por el ruido metálico del agua en la lata vacía. (34)
> Reconfortada por el sol de cobre...(23)

Earlier, 'El sol maduró. Pero ella no lo vio agonizar sobre las begonias' (20), which links the sun to images of rot to be discussed below. In the heat of the Sunday siesta, 'El río era una lámina de acero' (54). Related to this strand of images is that of other materials, some of which have already been noted: the Colonel's wife's stony breathing; 'su rostro parecía modelado en la materia de la hornilla' (63); 'Tengo el cerebro tieso como un palo' (20). However, the December weather makes the Colonel say, 'Se siente uno como si fuera de vidrio' (63), which is in direct contrast with his wife who 'se levantó impenetrable' (69), and with the 'hermetismo' that the Colonel encounters in Agustín's companions and in the doctor (39 and 59 respectively).

'El pueblo se hundió en el diluvio' (34); the drowned town belongs to a body of images associated with water, found in phrases such as: 'la pedregosa respiración de la mujer—remota—navegando en otro sueño' (34-35); 'El sirio Moisés...Era un oriental plácido forrado hasta el cráneo en una piel lisa y estirada, con densos movimientos de ahogado. Parecía efectivamente salvado de las aguas' (64); 'Un momento después estaba sumergido en la turbulenta atmósfera de la gallera' (64-65); 'insondable dulzura' (67). Water brings together the weather (October rains) and the geographical location (the only means of transportation is by river), and is an integral part of daily life, to the extent of becoming associated with, and giving a physical presence to, light: 'Los chorros de luz, la música estridente y los gritos de los niños oponían una resistencia física en el sector' (48).

The heat is also all-pervasive: 'El establecimiento hervía en la noche del domingo. El calor parecía más intenso a causa de las vibraciones del radio a todo volumen' (60); 'Era un mediodía ardiente. La oficina resplandecía con la reverberación de la calle. Embotado por el calor, el coronel cerró los ojos involuntariamente...El zumbido del ventilador eléctrico consolidó la penumbra. El coronel se sintió impaciente, atormentado por el sopor y por la bordoneante mujer...' (52-53). The oppressiveness of the heat is intensified by the mingling of heat, light and sound, so that there is no distinction between them.

As one would expect in a Catholic country like Colombia, religion is a strong influence on daily life, and religious terminology regularly occurs. As we saw in Chapter 3, the Colonel's wife uses the Catholic faith as a support, not only to give herself strength, but also to attack her husband: 'Es pecado quitarnos el pan de la boca para echárselo a un gallo' (37). Don

Sabas's wife also regards the Colonel's attitude to the cock as sinful ('—Una inyección para un gallo como si fuera un ser humano—gritó—. Eso es un sacrilegio', 44), but her remark does not carry the same weight because the impact of hunger is missing. The link between the Catholic concept of sin and starvation is reinforced by a description of the Colonel's wife in the final chapter: 'Masticó oraciones hasta un poco después del toque de queda' (70). Prayers are her food while she starves. Compare this with the irony of Don Sabas saying of artificial sweeteners, 'Es un martirio andar con esto por todas partes' (43).

The sound of the church bells in the novel has a dual function. The bells act as a spiritual stimulus to those like the Colonel's wife who say the Angelus (20), or they summon people to the funeral (3), or to Mass (16), but they also announce the moral censorship of films, which makes the priest and church instruments of political repression.

Humour is infused with religious expressions, for example: 'Éste es el milagro de la multiplicación de los panes' (23), discussed in more detail in Chapter 5 below. But there are also acceptable, non-Christian customs such as burying goods with the dead (the musician with his trumpet, 9), and fearing 'la mala hora' (37), and superstitions such as uncrossing cutlery (70), or 'Los maromeros comen gatos para no romperse los huesos' (64). Watching his wife, 'El coronel descubrió algo de irreal en su actitud, como si estuviera convocando para consultarlos a los espíritus de la casa' (21). Of this sentence, Pontiero says, 'as he watches his wife move about the house the Colonel is reminded of the melodramatic gestures of a medium' (*1*, p.xxvi). He could have added that the next sentence enhances this feeling with the image, 'puso la bomba sobre el altarcillo de litografías' (21-22); like a medium his wife seems capable of passing through walls (17), and she appears 'espectral' when lit from below (71). The Colonel's unchristian perception of her is at variance with her down-to-earthness.

Instead of seeing the religious terminology and imagery as part of a popular language found in any Catholic community, Graciela Maturo fashions an argument based on her belief that

García Márquez belongs to a Western tradition of metaphysical writing. The whole story, expressed in figurative language, is a symbol for the Christian calendar, starting at the October equinox (which, she says, is the commencement of the Advent period), progressing through spiritual regeneration to December (the month of the Nativity). Maturo also says that the forty-four days until the cockfight in January (71) is a reference to Lent and the Resurrection. Her parallels with, and details of, the Christian calendar are inexact; furthermore, to find, as she does, images of Job (who resists adversity and imposes dignity on poverty) and Christ in the Colonel, of Christ again in the cock, and of a sacrificial victim in Agustín, is suspect. There is no support for her premise that García Márquez is developing the Christian mystery of New Birth; the Colonel does not die, spiritually or physically. Moreoever, he does not relish the idea of eating 'mierda', even though Maturo says that the final word of the novel, which concludes an ending rich in signs of exultation and participation, is the most exultant word of all (*26*, pp.106-14).

The inhabitants of 'el pueblo' are obsessed by death, but in as much as death is a result of the violence that tyranny tries to make normal, the imagery of death stands for the political situation in which the town exists. Death appears as a fact of life: 'Lo único que llega con seguridad es la muerte, coronel' (46), 'La primera página estaba completamente ocupada por las invitaciones a un entierro' (15). It is entertainment, the film seen in 1931 was 'La voluntad del muerto' (34). The end result of cockfighting is death, but political repression inverts the normal run of events: Agustín, the cock's owner, is killed in the pit, while the cock appears to its new owner, the Colonel, the most alive thing he has ever held (66). At Agustín's death there would have been a great many spectators, but the witnesses are powerless to prevent such occurrences (similarly, the raid on the billiard hall is unopposed). Jacques Gilard states that in many of García Márquez's stories there are witnesses to a corpse (as at the musician's funeral), and the third-person narrative makes death, through the eyes of the characters, the main point of focus (*20*, p.19).

Pontiero says:

> Incipient death is written on the face of each and every
> member of this doomed community and the wailing
> mourners grouped around the dead musician's coffin
> contemplate 'el cadáver con la misma expresión con que se
> mira la corriente de un río' (8). The irresistible current of
> that imaginary river is the one moving force in this
> stagnant town. (*1*, xxvi-xxvii)

Apart from the fact that death is not written on everyone's face
(it pervades their thoughts, as with the wives of the Colonel and
Don Sabas), and that there are no wailing mourners (if there
were, 'De pronto empezó una voz...', 8, would go unnoticed),
'that imaginary river' does not fully clarify the image. It is, as
Bollettino says:

> precioso a pesar de lo trillado. La corriente no sólo
> representa la antigua metáfora desde Jorge Manrique, sino
> también la indiferencia, la apatía que muestran las mujeres
> hacia la muerte. Es decir, que la ironía del autor queda
> clara no sólo porque recurre al antiguo símil, sino por la
> actitud indiferente de las mujeres. (*10*, p.53)

As has been said above, the Colonel's wife is preoccupied with
death, Don Sabas's wife fantasises about it (44, 53), while her
husband regards carrying articifial sweeteners as 'como cargar la
muerte en el bolsillo' (43). If Don Sabas is fatalistic about
having diabetes, the Colonel is determined to survive his ill-
health:

> Agonizó muchas horas en el excusado...'Todo será
> distinto cuando acabe de llover.' Y lo creyó realmente,
> seguro de estar vivo en el momento en que llegara la carta.
> (35)

But, as Pontiero says:

> Death is the culmination of the many small deaths these characters have already suffered in the form of failure, sickness and bereavement and the image conveyed is of one final absurdity which obliterates a lifetime of empty actions. (*1*, p.xxvii)

The link between death and health is underlined by the references to rot. The Colonel's wife sums up the various levels of meaning of putrefaction: 'Nos estamos pudriendo vivos' (6). The humid climate includes rot ('Los almendros de la plaza soltaban sus últimas hojas podridas', 15; 'El sol maduró', 20); corruption is all around ('El mundo está corrompido', 16); Agustín said before his death, 'Cállate, que esta tarde nos vamos a podrir de plata' (37). In reality, the Colonel and his wife are anything but stinking rich (the only person who is is Don Sabas, and then by corrupt means); their position is encompassed by the rust in the coffee tin (3) and the excrement on which they will have to survive (73). Vargas Llosa points out that the beginning and the end of the novel sum up corrupt materialism and the carnality of the world (*34*, p.168). Rust, which even invades the brain ('Con este calor se oxidan las tuercas de la cabeza', 30), rots material from the outside, in comparison with excrement, which forms inside a body to be expelled as unwanted.

A fourth level of rot is the Colonel's feeling that he is rotting inside, described as fungus and poisonous plants growing in his gut (3, 35, 59). Commenting on the passage: 'Amaneció estragado. Al segundo toque para misa saltó de la hamaca...Entonces volvió al cuarto por el gallo' (16-17), Vargas Llosa says most of the elements of the Colonel's struggle are united: the cock, 'una realidad turbia', harshness which also contains optimistic connotations ('alborotada', and his innocent, trusting attitude), his constipation. His stomach acts as a link between the cock and the letter: '—¿Usted cree que darán ese dineral por el gallo?...Cuando salió de la oficina de don Sabas sentía una fuerte torcedura en las tripas, pero tenía conciencia de que esta vez no era a causa del tiempo...—Estoy esperando una carta urgente' (45-46). When his stomach gets better in December (whether because the climate has improved, or because, at the time, he has decided to sell the cock), he realises eventually that he will have to eat excrement. *Mierda* is therefore the counterweight to his hopes for the cock and the letter (*33*, pp.323-24).

In contrast with rot and, associated with it, the imagined plants in the Colonel's stomach, are living plants: 'Hasta donde alcanzaba su vista el pueblo estaba tapizado de flores' (7); ferns and begonias around the house (17, 20, 69), and grass and trees in the patio (62). Roses, on the other hand, are imaginary: in the picture in the Colonel's house (5), and 'Me gustaría sembrar las rosas' (62). But flowers are associated with death: 'la mujer llevó flores a la tumba de Agustín' (35); medicinal herbs with the Colonel's wife's sickness (36, 72), and Don Sabas's handkerchief is scented with lavender water, as an antidote to the 'pueblo de mierda' (45, 42). (The Colonel's wife scents her hair with lavender water, too, 23.)

Another type of natural imagery belongs to what Joset calls García Márquez's bestiary. The cock, as a symbol, has already been discussed. Other domestic birds appear: the duck and its brood in the lawyer's office (29), a hen crossing a deserted square (45), and an old hen brought to be mated with the cock (47). Other birds are mentioned: 'Yo siempre he dicho que su reloj anda con el de los gallinazos' (18), and 'El coronel volvió a reconocer a diciembre en el horario de los alcaravanes' (68), both of which are related to time.[21] Pigs and cats are mentioned indirectly (62, 64), while Don Sabas's castrated animals (52) contrast with the generative powers of the cock. Joset says 'Presumably there are circus animals' (p.70), but this is not the case: 'No es un circo de fieras', says the Colonel (64; unlike the circus that arrives in Macondo on the day that Colonel Aureliano Buendía dies, *5*, p.229). The Duke of Marlborough disguised as a tiger (16) belongs to a category called 'decoración animal' by Joset (p.71); one could also include the snake coiled around Don Sabas's and the black charlatan's neck (50, 66). Of

---

[21] Jacques Joset, 'El bestiario de Gabriel García Márquez', *Nueva Revista de Filología Hispánica*, 23 (1974), 65-87. On p.70, Joset lists all the occasions in García Márquez's work up to *Cien años de soledad* in which 'alcaravanes' tell the time.

the insects that appear, mosquitoes and worms have already been mentioned in relation to the weather and military imagery, flies come from the lavatory (17) and the musician's coffin (8), and fleas in the Colonel's wife's hair (23). There are a number of metaphorical animals, birds, insects and reptiles: 'Se necesita tener esa paciencia de buey que tú tienes' (26); 'ojos de murciélago' (61); 'Debo parecer un papagayo' (7); 'Pareces un pájaro carpintero' (20); the Colonel dreams of spiders' webs (17, 52); Don Sabas's eyes have 'una tristeza de sapo' (42). Joset points out two inverted metaphors related to animals: death 'es un animal con pezuñas' (44), and 'El único animal que se alimenta de carne humana es don Sabas' (59).

Whether real or metaphorical, animal references, like those to religion, come from a common fund of everyday terminology. It is not a question of 'harmony between the human and animal world' (*1*, p.xxxvii), but the juxtaposition of the environment with the characters' thoughts and actions. This occurs with the incongruous, but nevertheless real, passing of ducks through the lawyer's office; the equally incongruous concept of pigs eating roses, thus destroying the Colonel's wife's plans, but providing a source of humour ('Deben ser muy buenos los puercos engordados con rosas', 63). The hen that the apprentices bring to the cock is a cause of strife, but at the same time it inspires memories of Colonel Aureliano Buendía in better times (47). While the Colonel does achieve a great deal of rapport between himself and the cock, the same is not true of Don Sabas, who has animals castrated (52). Pontiero says that the association evoked by 'sapo' is greed, but toads are usually said to represent ingratiation (either is relevant to Don Sabas, though); and that 'culebra' evokes witchcraft, but, traditionally, snakes can also symbolize healing (hence the snake around the quack's neck). He calls the 'pajaritos de colores' (50) and the 'gato de yeso' (5) 'effigies...[which] suggest a keen interest in omens and symbols of good fortune among the town's inhabitants' (*1*, p.xxxvii). While the plaster cat is simply an ornament, the 'pajaritos de colores' are the same as the 'elefante dorado para colgarlo en la puerta' (21), what Joset calls metaphors of impossibilities (p.80).

Time, the importance of which as a theme is discussed in Chapter 2 above, is represented by prosaic objects, the buzzards and the curlews, and the clock. When the clock stops, it is set by the curfew bugle, linking it with the political theme; the Colonel and his wife try to sell the clock, but to no avail. With or without the clock, time, in the passing seconds, months, and years, in the natural 'clocks' of the curlews, and the unnatural ones (church bells, curfew), would continue progressing towards death.

In the tailor's shop, time is linked with musical imagery: 'Luego permaneció en silencio tamborileando sobre el envoltorio hasta cuando se dio cuenta de que alguien lo había advertido...''Ya está'', gritó Germán adentro, al tiempo con la campana del reloj' (39-40). (This also has political overtones because 'Había un letrero clavado sobre la guitarra: ''Prohibido hablar de política'' ', 40.) Once again, music is part of the general setting of 'el pueblo'. The popular songs of Rafael Escalona (38), the radio music in the billiard hall (60) and the band playing the funeral marches (despite missing its trumpet-player, 9), provide local colour. But music is related to a memory of happier times (the band playing at the festival in the past, 66), to humour ('Ya estoy encargado por una fábrica de clarinetes', 36), to death ('Uno de ellos inició en la armónica los acordes de una canción de moda. ''No toques hoy'', le dijo el coronel. ''Hay muerto en el pueblo'' ', 5), and to the lawyer's chaotic office ('La pianola sin teclas servía al mismo tiempo de escritorio', 28).

Entertainment is also provided by the circus, the first for ten years, and thus related to time and memory (64), and by gambling. The January cockfights are clearly a major event in the town's calendar; those of 1957 take on greater significance because they will be the first anniversary of Agustín's death. When the Colonel puts Agustín's cock in the pit, it will be the end of his parents' year of mourning, and (as has already been discussed) it will be of political importance to his colleagues. However, when the Colonel watches the roulette in the billiard hall, and suggests a losing number to Álvaro, he has an insight into gambling: 'Por primera vez experimentó la fascinación, el sobresalto y la amargura del azar' (61). Nevertheless, he retains a blind faith about winning. Having decided that the cock is not for sale, he denies to his wife the possibility of the cock losing:

—Entonces ya será veinte de enero—dijo el coronel, perfectamente consciente—. El veinte por ciento lo pagan esa misma tarde.
—Si el gallo gana—dijo la mujer—. Pero si pierde. No se te ha ocurrido que el gallo puede perder.
—Es un gallo que no puede perder. (72-73)

Just as he used to believe that a letter would come, he now believes in the cock's victory. While those around him gamble with money, the Colonel, who is penniless, but prepared to stake his future, refuses to admit that he is committing his own and his wife's life to one afternoon of chance.

One final source of imagery, drawn from the entertainments in 'el pueblo', is the cinema. We have seen how the Colonel appears as on a cinema screen to his wife, and how the censorship of films relates the church to political repression. Of the poster advertising the film *Virgen de medianoche* (48), Pontiero says 'Prurience and sensationalism tend to be the main features of the poor-quality films shown in remote provincial towns throughout Latin America' (*1*, p.xxi, n.12). The other film, *La voluntad del muerto*, sounds equally melodramatic: 'El aguacero se desgajó cuando el fantasma trataba de robarle el collar a la muchacha' (34). These film fantasies have nothing to do with harsh reality, but the two titles suggest that, as far as the cinema is concerned, nothing has changed in twenty-five years (*La voluntad del muerto* was shown in 1931, that is one year after the festival that the Colonel remembers).

The intertwining of different strands of imagery shows the close relationship between many factual and metaphorical elements which in turn underlines the oppressive atmosphere of the town in the winter months and during a time of political repression. Pontiero says:

The combined effect in the novel of external forces such as the fierce climate, political repression, isolation and fears rooted as much in superstition as in orthodox religious beliefs, is to distort and sometimes even displace reality. (*1*, p.xxiii)

He calls the distorted perception 'hallucinated visions'. While there is an imaginative aspect to the Colonel's feeling of floating in gelatine, leading to his feverish memory of his revolutionary past, including a vision of the Duke of Marlborough (16), or to experiencing plants in his intestines, these and the other examples that Pontiero cites are what he correctly calls 'logical exaggerations of real situations'. They are not deprived of all objectivity (which is the meaning of hallucination). Regarding the weather, Pontiero says it causes 'physical and mental disorders—somnolence, amnesia, fever, malaria and insanity', none of which is hallucinatory (*1*, p.xxiii); 'nature behaves perversely: "La humedad continuaba pero no llovía" (7)—the laws of cause and effect no longer in evidence', on the contrary, it is a perfectly natural phenomenon for it to be humid without rain falling. Furthermore, Pontiero says that the sudden appearance of 'un vaho de moscas triangulares' (17) suggests some omen or premonition, which is hastily dismissed by the Colonel as a false alarm (*1*, p.xxiv); this is not a strange vision, as one might expect flies to emerge from beneath the lavatory lid in a hot climate. Besides, it is not the flies that represent a false alarm, but his desire to empty his bowels, as the next sentence demonstrates: 'Acuclillado en la plataforma de tablas sin cepillar experimentó la desazón del anhelo frustrado' (17).

Pontiero uses 'puercos engordados con rosas' as an example of a strange perception of a world in a state of transformation (*1*, p.xxiv). It is a strange perception, but the world is not being transformed in any sense other than by the Colonel's humorous reaction to his wife's defeatism. He shows the same type of imaginative and responsive humour when talking of his shoes to Alfonso: 'Estos monstruos tienen cuarenta años y es la primera vez que oyen una mala palabra' (40). Again, the holed umbrella is useful for counting stars (5-6); this is not strictly a magical property for umbrellas (*1*, p.xxvi), but a brand-new use, including humour, unique possibilities and different levels of meaning. Just as an undamaged clown's umbrella is a prop for its user's antics, so, eaten by moths, it becomes a medium for the author. It captures the Colonel's memory of the past, better times; in its physical form ('un misterioso sistema de varillas metálicas'), it becomes an unrecognisable object. It shows that, although unable to fulfil its original function, it has a new function, that of inspiring humour tinged with sadness: counting stars is an image of unattainability.

Although García Márquez uses a direct, impersonal style for his narrative, terms such as the marvellous real (subject to disciplining, *24*, p.17) and magic realism (*1*, p.xli) are applied to it.[22] The latter is in fact irrelevant, despite the Colonel saying, 'La vida es la cosa mejor que se ha inventado' (46). This must be a literary joke because there is no invention imposed upon reality. The novel has a contrapuntal technique (to be discussed in the next chapter), the aim of which is:

> fundir en una unidad narrativa situaciones o datos que ocurren en tiempo y/o espacio diferentes o que son de naturaleza distinta, para que esas realidades se enriquezcan mutuamente, modificándose, fundiéndose en una nueva realidad, distinta de la simple suma de sus partes. (*33*, p.322)

Vargas Llosa's new realism of juxtaposition differs from the neorealism of which Bollettino speaks:

> Tampoco podemos pensar que el escritor colombiano esté siguiendo la técnica surrealista al subrayar objetos aislados, porque las asociaciones y las descripciones de los objetos no son aisladas ni deformed. Lo que sí tenemos en Gabriel García Márquez es un nerorrealismo, un deseo de

---

[22] The distinction between marvellous reality and magic realism is that in the former the artist finds creative stimulus in the natural conjunction in the New World of objects that should never be found together, while magic realism reaffirms the writer's right to invent reality, to make up his story rather than copy what he observes. See John S. Brushwood, *The Spanish American Novel: A Twentieth-Century Survey* (Austin: University of Texas Press, 1975), pp.172-73; also Alejo Carpentier, 'De lo real maravilloso americano', in *Tientos y diferencias* (Montevideo: Editorial Arca, 1967), pp.103-21.

captar la realidad de manera concisa sin que intervengan sentimientos de los personajes. (*10*, p.52; compare this with Pontiero's assertion that 'The dreams and nightmares of the town's inhabitants have all the panache and extravagance of surrealism', *1*, p.xxiv)

Undoubtedly, concision and unsentimentality are important features in the text, but Bollettino goes on to say that the presentation of objects imprisons the imagination so that the reader is confronted with a photographic reality which has no power of association with any other reality (*10*, p.63). He overstresses their prosaic nature by failing to distinguish between photographic and cinematographic reality. The difference is important:

> Of all the technical properties of film the most general and indispensable is editing. It serves to establish a meaningful continuity of shots and is therefore unthinkable in photography.[23]

García Márquez says:

> compruebo ahora que en todos mis libros anteriores a *Cien años de soledad* hay un inmoderado afán de visualización de los personajes y las escenas, y hasta una obsesión por indicar puntos de vista y encuadres.
> —Estás pensando, sin duda, en *El coronel no tiene quien le escriba*.
> —Sí, es una novela cuyo estilo parece el de un guión cinematográfico. Los movimientos de los personajes son como seguidos por una cámara. Y cuando vuelvo a leer el libro, veo la cámara. Hoy creo que las soluciones literarias son diferentes a las soluciones cinematográficas. (*28*, p.45)

The intervening years have probably given the author this rather

[23] Siegfried Kracauer, *Theory of Film: The Redemption of Physical Reality* (New York: Oxford University Press, 1960), p.29.

dismissive view of *El coronel*; the book is not so steeped in film
techniques that the reader feels he ought to be seeing it in the
cinema, despite Bollettino's statement: 'Gabriel García Márquez
entra abruptamente en la acción sin preámbulo. Las luces del
cine se apagan y en la pantalla empieza a tomar forma la figura
del coronel preparándose un café' (*10*, p.49).

In individual scenes, the numerous points of view suggest
camera angles; the detached eye of the omnipresent narrator
places various shots together to provide the complete image
through montage (see p.88 below). Both McMurray and
Pontiero mention the camera techniques of close-up, speed-up
and fade out. McMurray quotes the scene at the funeral of the
musician (*25*, p.30). An instance from this scene, in which the
viewpoint zooms in from the distant to the close-up, is:

Pero alguien le puso una mano en la espalda, lo empujó
hacia el fondo del cuarto por una galería de rostros
perplejos hasta el lugar donde se encontraban—profundas
y dilatadas—las fosas nasales del muerto. (8)

Pontiero gives further examples: 'El coronel permaneció inmóvil
en el centro de la oficina...la única cosa móvil en el pueblo' (54),
which 'builds up a hypnotic picture of solitude and immobility',
and 'Don Sabas no soportó más...Una gallina de largas patas
amarillas atravesaba la plaza desierta' (44-45), 'a veritable *mise
en scène* with a subtle contrast of gesture and mood' (*1*, pp.xxxv-
xxxvi).[24]

García Márquez's admission of a debt to the cinema does not
make *El coronel* a progression of cinematographic images,
excluding literary qualities. As García Márquez himself says:

En efecto, la realidad en la literatura no es fotográfica sino

[24] It is interesting to note that while everybody in 'el pueblo' goes to the cinema
(if custom allows), in Macondo, the cinema, together with the public
gramophone and other places of entertainment, is either one of the 'diversiones
para la hojarasca' (i.e. not for decent folk), or 'una máquina de ilusión que no
merecía los desbordamientos pasionales del público' (*3*, p.73 and *5*, p.194
respectively). The latter quotation exemplifies the fact that *Cien años de soledad*
was written as a celebration of the limitless possibilities of the novel in contrast
with the relative narrowness of the cinema (see *18*, p.38 or *16*, p.33).

sintética, y encontrar los elementos esenciales para esa
síntesis es uno de los secretos del arte de narrar. (*28*, p.184)

The constant interlinking of themes, symbols and images (hardly
any of which have their roots outside the framework of the text),
and the precise use of language and humour raise the use of
imagery above the level of mere pictures. García Márquez takes
advantage of cinematographic techniques because 'The motion-
picture camera has a way of disintegrating familiar objects and
bringing to the fore—often in just moving about—previously
invisible interrelationships between parts of them.'[25] It is in this
way that the author can heighten brutal reality by exaggerating it
at times, making it appear extraordinary so that 'A veces
suceden cosas muy extrañas' (44), without losing the detached
eye necessary to express the biographical, social and political
themes that he seeks to convey.

[25] Kracauer, *Theory of Film*, p.54.

5 *Style*

El coronel no tiene quien le escriba is written in third-person narrative. At no point does the narrator impose his presence on the story; he is, in Regina Janes's words, 'effaced' (*24*, p.16). One of the traditional attributes of this type of narrator is omniscience; while the narrator describes the events of the story in linear fashion, he has the power to enter the characters' minds, interpolate their memories and hopes for the future, and disclose the ironies that lurk beneath their actions and thoughts.

A compliment often paid by critics to the style of *El coronel* is that, through an exact use of words, the maximum force is achieved with a minimum of expression. There are numerous examples; of verbs: 'Álvaro se obstinó en perder' (60), and of verbs and nouns: 'Masticó oraciones' (70), 'los ojos apoyados en el saco del correo' (24), 'buscando el aire' (70; and 'buscar el aire', 9), 'no le arrancó una lágrima' (70); of nouns and adjectives: 'una desolación aplicada' (58), 'Los viajeros descendieron estragados' (13), 'El viscoso aire de octubre' (68), 'insondable dulzura' (67); of adverbs: 'hablando sordamente' (71), 'había caído fatalmente en una batida' (61), 'estaba perfectamente vivo' (37). Apart from the mutual reinforcement of meaning in the precise placement of words, the exactitude is used for categoric definition and the eradication of opinions (*29*, p.60). The oppressive reality of the environment is found not only in the nouns and verbs and their qualifiers (for instance, the rain that falls 'implacablemente', 45), but also, as Rolfe notes, in the insistence on concrete objects through the use of the definite article (*31*, p.342). Within this concrete world the characters are isolated; as Bollettino says:

> faltan las descripciones en que se hace patente el estado de ánimo de los personajes en relación con su contorno. Hubiera caído fácilmente en un sentimentalismo barato si

se hubiera identificado con sus protagonistas. (*10*, p.52)

The lack of sentimentality will appear below in relation to dialogue and humour, but it is not so rigid as to prohibit the characters from voicing opinions about their fellows.

As has been mentioned above in Chapter 3, descriptions of characters are brief, concentrating usually on particular aspects of anatomy, habit or dress in order to emphasise personality traits. Vargas Llosa calls this a technique of formulae (*33*, p.327). The Colonel, as we have seen, is faceless, and is described through recurring actions, while his wife is character-ized by her asthmatic breathing and her preoccupation with death. The doctor's hair and particularly his teeth (14, 19, 57) are his essential features. Don Sabas is described as 'the perfect image of self-indulgence and misery' (42; *1*, p.xxxv). Even the briefest descriptions are informative, such as the policeman who confronts the Colonel: 'Era pequeño, aindiado, de piel curtida, y exhalaba un tufo infantil' (61). This takes in size, race, colouring and demeanour. His childish air, which echoes the boy who pointed his wooden gun at the Colonel (48), has a more poignant significance because he shot Agustín.

Physical description, in every case but that of Don Sabas, commences 'Era...': the Colonel's wife (4), the Colonel himself (7), the doctor (14), the lawyer (27), Álvaro (38), Don Sabas's wife (44), the policeman (61), and Moisés (64). It is always a direct approach on the physical level (and equally so in Don Sabas's case when an incomplete sentence is used). Every person is seen when in communication verbally or visually with another. Further information is added during the characters' inter-actions, for instance: 'Su indolente manera de actuar exasperaba al coronel' (14). A picture is constructed from initial narrative fact to the narrator providing information given by the characters themselves.

'Era...' is also used as a direct, factual supplier of temporal or climatic information: 'Era octubre' (3); 'Era una tarde lúcida' (15). Although there is a greater range of expressions for atmo-sphere, none of which is extended (for example: 'La humedad fue sustituida por el sopor', 23), many are linked to time

('Escampó después de las nueve', 7; 'Llovió toda la semana', 35), or suggest time themselves ('El sol maduró', 20; 'El sol avanzó', 30).

Only a minimum of details is given in descriptions of place. Although we are told that the town has a river, a square, flowers (7), dusty almond trees (15, 42) and various buildings, its exact layout is unknown, and none of its particulars is provided at once, only when the Colonel walks through the town for some purpose. The Colonel's house is at the edge of town (7) and is described from the inside out, with the clock as the centre of focus in the living room (3-7). In contrast to Don Sabas's house, of which we do not get the full picture except that it has two storeys (11, 50), is cluttered (42), has electricity (for its fan), and is his town house besides his 'finca' (56), we discover that what is described of the Colonel's house is all that he and his wife have. They have sold their major possessions, and are prepared to sell the little they have left.

Descriptions of character, atmosphere and place are given in few words to produce an immediate visual effect. To these are added repetitive sounds: the church bells, for services or censorship, the curfew bugle, the weekly whistle of the launches, the rain on the roof (34), the drop of water falling into a tin (16, 34), the 'minucioso cuchicheo' (17), music (the funeral marches, the strident radio in the billiard hall), shouts (again at the funeral, at the cockpit, and of Don Sabas, mingling with the screams of castrated animals). Bollettino says that there are 'olores insoportables que el autor logra evocar con frases breves que detienen la sensación y aumentan la tensión' (*10*, p.54). Of the smells that are mentioned, only 'sombríos olores' and 'el vapor amoniacal del bacinete' (17), and Don Sabas's urine (56) could be said to be unpleasant, but none is described as unbearable. Other smells are 'el olor de muchas flores diferentes' (8), 'su traje de lino intachable exhalaba un hálito de frescura' (18), 'un vaho de hierbas medicinales' (36, 72). Of the suggested smells (insecticide, 16, 21; lavender water, 23, 45; flowers, coffee, rot) only the latter would be unbearable, but it is never given olfactory connotations. While Pontiero correctly equates all the senses with the 'náuseas' that the Colonel feels in October (17), the stench of the month (*1*, p.xxxvi) is only implied through the need for perfume or medicines to ease breathing in the 'aire viscoso de octubre' (68), in the same way that heat is suggested by references to fanning (24, 28, 42, 52). However, one smell from outside 'el pueblo' impinges on the Colonel's present, his recollection of the smell of bananas (51). That smell upset his stomach, but in realising that half a century later he has had no peace, he is aware that the stagnation of 'el pueblo', everpresent death, and the annual torture of October weather on his guts, allow no respite from bitter reality. Similarly, a sound from his past assails him, the big drum beating at a fund-raising festival of years ago. This too acts on his stomach, mournfully; its recollection is stimulated by the sounds of the crowd in the cockpit who, until his cock was put in the ring, had existed in 'una especie de sopor' (66). This 'sopor' had been made evident by the constant references to silence, silent streets, motionless-ness. These two memories, and the sounds of the launches, are rare instances of the closed world of 'el pueblo' being infiltrated by the outside.

The closed environment is emphasized in the 'hermetismo insólito' of the doctor (59), the 'rostros herméticos' of the apprentices (39), the 'inasible' Colonel and his 'insondable dulzura' (67) and 'impenetrable noche' (16); it is also reflected in the novel's structure. *El coronel*, as a complete unit, refers to events outside itself in time (or to other novels and stories by García Márquez, which are also temporal because, fictitious or not, they are historic). Theoretically, the possibilities inspired by *El coronel* go on at least until the cockfight in January, 1957. But the novel is made up of inconclusive scenes which, linked with the constant waiting, give the impression of time being static, so that the lack of a conclusion provides no future momentum. It is immaterial whether the cock wins or not because its victory or defeat will not change the overall state of affairs. It is a book, as García Márquez himself says, that ends on the last page (*28*, p.82).

The novel is divided into seven sections; each is a self-contained unit highlighting one, or a few, instances from the life of the characters under scrutiny. Just as the novel starts *in medias res* and ends inconclusively, so does each chapter. For example, the fifth chapter begins abruptly: 'Espérese y le presto un paraguas, compadre' (42). There is no introductory statement that it is raining, nor that the Colonel is in Don Sabas's office; the only clue is 'compadre', which was used by the two men in the first chapter. This chapter ends:

> —La cuestión del gallo —dijo el coronel—. Mañana mismo se lo vendo a mi compadre Sabas por novecientos pesos. (51)

This concludes the Colonel's and his wife's discussion, but looks forward to the next day. Within the setting of persistent elements (waiting and routine, the weather, implied violence), such inconclusive scenes create tension.

The chapters are linked by overlapping elements. Pontiero indicates the interlocking of recurrent themes (the letter, the cock, Agustín, the lost years), which alternate expectation with uncertainty and suspense with pathos (*1*, p.xxxii). Castagnino shows the links between the chapters as follows: between the first and second, the cock; the second and third, misery and poverty; the third and fourth, the letter to change lawyers; the fourth and fifth, and fifth and sixth, domestic misery; and between the sixth and seventh, a synthesis of all the foregoing (*11*, p.28; on pp.87-103 he gives a detailed structural analysis of each chapter).

The chapters refer backward and forward within the text, as exemplified by the beginning of the third chapter (23-24). It opens with an ironic joke relating to the theme of poverty, plus an indicator of time ('la semana siguiente'), and a reference to the previous chapter (the wife's skill at patching and mending). After the week, we are told the month, October, here associated with a military image ('la tregua'), and what the weather is like, a constant factor. A new action is introduced, the wife doing her hair, normally an ordinary act which here assumes much importance. The religious joke on the time the hairdo takes balances the opening sentence. It connects with the Colonel's haircut a few lines later. When he examines his head with his hands we are reminded of his anonymity (he has no mirror, see

Chapter 3 above), and of his concern for how he looks to other
people ('Debo parecer un papagayo', 7). Although his haircut is
of less duration it has even greater significance than his wife's
hairdo; on the one hand it inspires the impossible temporal joke,
'Me has quitado veinte años de encima' (his wife's reaction
harks back to her response to his fear of looking like a parrot,
7). On the other hand, his wife is inspired to say, 'Cuando estoy
bien soy capaz de resucitar un muerto' (24), which has the
bitterly ironic suggestion behind it that their son cannot be
revived, and they both know it.

The hairdo and the haircut are split by a few lines which
contain references to the theme of waiting, to the cock,
specifically to its future (first in the Colonel's worry, then in the
optimism of Agustín's companions), and time is seen to pass
rapidly. After the Colonel's haircut, his wife saddens. The
repeated poverty theme ('Ya no quedaba en la casa nada que
vender, salvo el reloj y el cuadro') refers to later when she and
her husband try to exchange the clock and picture for money.
On Thursday night the wife is desperately concerned about their
situation, which compares with the Colonel worrying about the
cock on Tuesday (23). Her husband says: 'No te preocupes',
which is echoed later in the chapter when the lawyer says, 'no
hay que desesperarse' (28). (Though the lawyer himself despairs
at the Colonel's attitude, 31.) 'Mañana viene el correo', says the
Colonel (24); this is a major theme, referring to before the text,
to the previous, and to future, chapters.

The references to time direct the narrative on the temporal
plane. On the spatial plane, there is not as much definition. The
narrative method is akin to cinematic cutting.[26] We only know
that Agustín's colleagues have visited when we are told that they
are going (23). We do not see the Colonel go for the post, we
simply see him waiting at the doctor's office (24). The postman
speaks as he departs. The focus is switched to the Colonel, who
does not take the road home, but goes to the tailor's. His

[26] See Seymour Chatman, *Story and Discourse: Narrative Structure in Fiction
and Film* (Ithaca: Cornell University Press, 1978), pp.101-02, on the creation of
movement through editing and the coincidence in literary and film methods in
the creation of space.

journey is not shown; we only see him at the shop taking coffee while the apprentices read magazines. The tailor's shop closes; cut to the Colonel's house where his wife is waiting. The one-word repeated dialogue is forceful and abrupt. No reaction to 'nada' is given. Instead the scene cuts to the Colonel returning to the launches a week later and immediately cuts again to him going home with no letter. The Colonel's first empty-handed return is charged with his emotion: 'Se sentía defraudado'; he is unwilling to face reality. These acquire more power because they, and the afternoon in which they are felt, are described more fully than the movements that surround them. Further-more, by showing time but not movement, the ritual of returning to the post on Fridays is compressed, so that the Colonel's despair applies to any Friday rather than a particular one (26).

The effect of cutting rapidly from one scene to another, stressing passing time and implying motion, is to create an irregular but nonetheless relentless rhythm. A smooth flow in the narrative is further prevented by placing together sentences of varying length. Take, for example: 'El no encontró la voz para responder...y encontró a su mujer remendando entre las begonias' (69). The first sentence refers to the night-time, the second to dawn and the Colonel's eventual sleep. Continuing with the topic of sleep, the third and fourth sentences show him waking and his wife sleeping, but each sentence has a different subject: in the third it is the sun; in the fourth, his wife. The fifth sentence returns to the the Colonel whom we see going about his daily routine, which includes waiting. In the second paragraph, the jerkiness continues: she awakens; they say good morning and sit down; the Colonel has breakfast; he passes the morning in a new situation (with no sign of movement). At a precise time, one o'clock, he returns home (motion is indicated). The rhythm is irregular, but not arbitrarily so. Each sentence gives no more information than is necessary, but the sum appears to cover all possible angles of the scene, in both time and space. This staccato effect takes place within the overall momentum of the Colonel having to find a solution to his problems, but which, at the end, stops. 'Es un ritmo que no sólo se mueve dentro de un

límite sino que también va tomando volumen a medida que el
espacio en que se mueve el protagonista se empequeñece' (*10*,
p.62).

Usually the Colonel's memories are told in continuous prose
of long sentences (5-6, 29, 31, 66). That on page 51 is broken by
short sentences: 'Era la fiebre del banano. "Me voy", dijo
entonces el coronel. "El olor del banano me descompone los
intestinos."' Memory normally comes easily to the old man,
and compared to the fragmented present, can be expressed in a
flowing way. However, the banana fever was such a disruptive
event in his life that it is told in the same way as the continually
unsettling present.

Repetition as a structural effect is used to evoke the static
nature of life: temporal phrases, the weather, reiterated images
or types of images. For the Colonel and his wife the frequent use
of 'descubrir, darse cuenta, acordarse, encontrar, advertir'
underlines the temporary forgetfulness that waiting inflicts upon
them, or how its numbing effect is relieved by sudden, surprising
facts springing to their attention. To emphasize the temporal
nature, such words are often linked with a phrase 'sólo
entonces': 'Sólo entonces se acordó del gallo amarrado a la pata
de la cama' (4); 'Sólo entonces descubrió el circo' (64). Pontiero
says (perhaps overstating the desperation):

> The reiteration of verbs like: *traducir, descifrar, identificar*
> and *intuir* underlines the pervading note of bewilderment
> and frenzied speculation and this is further emphasised by
> a constant mutation of mental states ranging from
> *distraído* and *ausente* to *concentrado* and *absorto*; from
> *exultado* to *alucinado*. (*1*, p.xxxvii)

In the same way that descriptions are given formulaic treatment, so certain set phrases appear in the sentence structure. The
use of 'Era...' has already been mentioned, and is an obvious
example. Temporal clauses are emphasized by placing the
adverb or preposition at the beginning of the sentence. In a
similar position, 'Así que...' is used to provide a scene change
('Así que el sábado en la tarde el coronel fue a visitar a su

abogado', 27; 'Así que fue a darlo esa noche', 48). Informative phrases are allowed to gain greater objectivity by being isolated: 'De manera que el coronel tuvo que decidirse por el viejo traje de paño negro que después de su matrimonio sólo usaba en ocasiones especiales' (5). There are also sentences with no verb, either as lists of details:

> Botines de charol, pantalón blanco sin correa y la camisa sin cuello postizo, cerrada arriba con el botón de cobre. (13)

> Colgados en la parte superior, media docena de paraguas y una sombrilla de mujer. (42)

> Al fondo, amontonados en desorden, sacos de sal, pellejos de miel y sillas de montar. (42)

or of a specific detail:

> En la pared opuesta a la del reloj, el cuadro de una mujer entre tules rodeada de amorines en una barca cargada de rosas. (5)

> Revelaciones sobre el estado de la resistencia armada en el interior del país. (18)

A large number of sentences being with 'Pero...'. In conversation it can denote argument, particularly in the lawyer's office. Although 'pero' is used by the Colonel and his wife on page 73, this is not a general rule because their conversations are often a series of antithetical statements. In common usage, the conjunction *but* demonstrates contrast between two sets of actions or states. In this simple form, we find: 'Pero su marido no le puso atención' (4), but often in *El coronel* 'pero' introduces a note of reality: 'Pero la insistencia de los bronces rotos le recordó el entierro' (4); 'Pero antes de las doce había recobrado su densidad, su peso humano' (17). More obviously, 'Pero cuando cerraron la sastrería tuvo que hacerle frente a la realidad' (26); 'Pero en realidad estaba apenas sostenido por la esperanza de la carta' (36); 'Pero en realidad se sentía amargado' (51). The placement of 'pero' at the beginning of a separate clause rather than in a subordinate clause gives a far greater sense of contrast.

Contrast is an integral part of the text. Pontiero notes this, singling out the contrast, both physical and spiritual, between the Colonel and Don Sabas, and the contrast in the conflicting traits within the Colonel's character (*1*, p.xxxiii). Talking of García Márquez's style, Gullón mentions four condensing techniques which contain elements of contrast: paradox (a self-contradictory statement: 'sudor helado', 16); anachronism (something out of keeping with chronology: the Duke of Marlborough appearing in the War of a Thousand Days, 16); oxymoron (contradicting terms linked in a phrase: 'hablando sordamente', 71); synaesthesia (applying to an object qualities it does not have: 'dolor sordo', 17; 'densos movimientos', 64); oxymoron and synaesthesia mixed: 'El gallo produjo un sonido gutural que llegó hasta el corredor como una sorda conversación humana' (47; see *22*, p.153; my examples).

Contrast occurs in the paragraph structure:

> El coronel permaneció inmóvil en el centro de la oficina hasta cuando acabó de oír las pisadas de los dos hombres en el extremo del corredor...El coronel se dirigió a su casa con la certidumbre de ser la única cosa móvil en el pueblo. (54)

To borrow Pontiero's words, there are 'balanced structures and symmetrical detail' (*1*, p.xxxiii). Contrasts occur over longer stretches of narration. For example: 'En la segunda quincena de noviembre creyó que el animal se moriría después de dos días sin maíz.' The Colonel remembers some beans which he gives to the cock. His attention to the bird prompts his wife to think of Agustín's death, then she and her husband continue on the subject of death (36). During this protracted conversation, the Colonel says:

—Nadie se muere en tres meses...Pero si nos fuéramos a morir de hambre ya nos hubiéramos muerto.

El gallo estaba perfectamente vivo frente al tarro vacío. (37)

Not only is there a contrast between life and death, but the dead Agustín is juxtaposed with the living cock that once belonged to him (which is 'perfectamente vivo', as if there could be no possible thought of its death despite its new owner's earlier fears). The couple's hunger and possible death is juxtaposed with the cock's empty tin, it having just eaten. This contrast reappears in the final chapter when the Colonel feels the life in the bird (66). The threat of death remains, though, in the cockpit, and especially for himself and his wife since he has just decided not to sell the cock.

Juxtapositions are created by the impersonal narration when an action is broken by a description of the weather:

Un momento después el abogado revolvió el despacho en busca del poder. El sol avanzó hacia el centro de la escueta habitación construida con tablas sin cepillar. Después de buscar inútilmente por todas partes, el abogado se puso a gatas, bufando, y cogió un rollo de papeles bajo la pianola. (30)

Alternatively, the weather begins a new paragraph in the middle of a scene:

—12 de agosto 1949.

Un momento después empezó a llover. El coronel llenó una hoja de garabatos grandes, un poco infantiles. (33)

Juxtapositions also arise from the deliberate linking of different ideas. This provokes contrasts (as seen in the stylistic figures mentioned above), but it can also produce surprises. Pontiero says:

There are numerous examples of binary arrangements of

nouns and adjectives designed to create a special emphasis, while subtle juxtapositions of images provoke unexpected associations. (*I*, p.xxxiii)

While one would not disagree with Pontiero's judgement of ternary arrangements,[27] his examples of binary groupings show emphasis, but do not clarify the use of juxtaposition (*I*, p.xxxiv). 'En el mar hay *barcos anclados* en permanente contacto con los *aviones nocturnos*' (25; Pontiero's italics) is not an unexpected association; its effect comes from the comparison of the safety of flying with the precariousness of the launch journey. During this extended juxtaposition, an image is introduced that does appear extraordinary in relation to the conversation and the scene, but which is quite apt: 'Debe ser como las alfombras' (25). On the one hand, 'permanente contacto' and 'más seguro' of the doctor's previous speech suggest the position of a carpet on the floor. But planes fly at 20,000 feet, a figure that the Colonel cannot conceive (24), so his perplexity expresses itself in terms of magic carpets.

In the passage 'Don Sabas carraspeó...Cuando don Sabas lo empujó hacia la pared para dar paso a los hombres que transportaban al muerto, volvió su cara sonriente hacia él, pero se encontró con un rostro duro' (9-10), there are many juxtaposed elements. Sounds contrast with silences: 'conversar...grito...los músicos suspendieron la marcha...la voz del padre Ángel conversando a gritos...la crepitación de la lluvia sobre el paraguas...en silencio...lanzaron gritos de alabanzas, de gratitud y despedida, como si creyeran que el muerto las escuchaba dentro del ataúd.' These last shouts are not what one would expect at a wake. Within this is the confrontation of the mayor with the funeral cortège, in itself not too unusual, given the state of siege (which is referred to after the mayor's

---

[27] Among the examples given by Pontiero of ternary arrangements are: 'Eres caprichoso, terco y desconsiderado, repitió ella' (70), a trenchant description of an individual personality; 'El coronel observó la confusión de rostros cálidos, ansiosos, terriblemente vivos' (65), dramatizing the scene; and examples that create a note of crisis or suspense ('se sintió tragado por esos ojos, triturado, digerido e inmediatamente expulsado', 61), or convey a sense of prodigy and excess (for example, 'su asombrosa habilidad para componer, zurcir y remendar', 23). See *I*, p.xxxiv.

interruption), except that the mayor 'Estaba en calzoncillos y franela, hinchada la mejilla sin afeitar'. His appearance is out of keeping with his authoritarian stand and makes an already petty regulation absurd.

Angel Rama says that each event, each piece of dialogue has a certain autonomy and that the resulting fragmented narrative enhances the static atmosphere (*29*, p.62). However, in Castagnino's view, there is strict organization of narrative voice and direct and indirect speech. In places, such as when the Colonel is reading the paper's headlines, the narrative voice and the Colonel's reading are one and the same (*11*, p.161). But when the narrative voice disrupts, or is broken by, dialogue, tension is created. For instance:

> Recostó el taburete contra el marco de la puerta y se sentó a esperar que Álvaro quedara solo para proponerle el negocio...El alemán le arranca diez pesos y se lo deja lo mismo. (39)

Tension is initiated by saying that the Colonel is waiting for Álvaro alone. This is continued by broken dialogue, especially 'Quedó en suspenso'. His lie and evasion to Germán, and another silence, heighten the tension further. Eventually, the Colonel gives in, omitting to say that the clock is for sale. As a result, nothing is resolved, even though the outcome is that the apprentices will feed the cock.

Most of the speech in the novel is direct; indirect speech is a résumé, usually in one or two words, of the overall sentiment of what has been said. For example: 'Ellos protestaron' (39); 'El coronel rehusó el ofrecimiento' (40); 'El sirio Moisés verificó la información' (64). Each section of direct dialogue is realistic, being clipped and containing humour, bitterness, irony, indifference. García Márquez, in following his friend Vinyes' advice of 'Intenta escribir como hablas', has achieved a naturalness in the style of *El coronel*, which, as Pontiero points out, is most obvious in the dialogue (*1*, pp.xxxviii-xxxix).

Returning from the dock, the Colonel and the doctor discuss what is in the papers. The brief exchange:

—Qué hay de noticias —preguntó el coronel.
El médico le dio varios periódicos.
—No se sabe —dijo—. Es difícil leer entre líneas lo que
permite publicar la censura...
—No hay esperanzas de elecciones —dijo el coronel.
—No sea ingenuo, coronel —dijo el médico—. Ya
nosotros estamos muy grandes para esperar al Mesías. (15)

of itself straightforward, gives the impression of being isolated
because it is preceded by a short paragraph that not only says
that the two men are returning from the dock to the doctor's
office in the late afternoon (suggesting spatial and temporal
movement), but also, in describing the two men as they walk,
gives the strongest of disjunctive phrases in terms of speech: 'en
silencio'. In fact, these four exchanges are firmly rooted in many
elements within the story and do not stand alone. 'Qué hay de
noticias' is a question, but it has no interrogation marks. The
Colonel's wife is obliged to 'preguntar afirmando' because of
her asthma (4), but many of the Colonel's questions do have
question marks (see his questions to her, 48-49). Here, though, it
is a conditioned response to someone reading the newspapers to
ask what is new, but just as the Colonel has come to expect no
information from clandestine leaflets (18), he asks without
expecting anything. His pessimism is confirmed by the doctor's
reply, which adds one of the few direct references to the political
situation (that censorship is in force). This is enlarged upon by
an intervening paragraph on the paper's content, including Suez
(mentioned again, 25) and invitations to a burial. The latter
harks back to the musician's funeral, and provokes the idea that
this burial may be for someone who died of unnatural causes.
'No hay esperanzas de elecciones' maintains the political theme,
with a hint of a question, but chiefly despair. The first half of
the doctor's reply employs the word 'ingenuo' (repeated, 59) as a
specific reminder of a few lines earlier: 'Volvió hacia el médico
una mirada enteramente infantil' (14). It also underlines the
attitude that most people have towards the Colonel, but which,
as was shown in Chapter 3 above, is not absolutely correct.
In extending the idea and tone of infantility to everyone ('Ya

nosotros estamos muy grandes...'), the doctor reveals his own character, frustrated and cynical. Pontiero's remark on this statement is not wholly correct. True, the doctor sums up the collective sense of frustration, but there is no evidence of the opposition being 'defeated once more in rigged elections' (*1*, p.xxiii). Also, his footnote 15 implies that 'Mesías' refers by association to a liberator, but the doctor regards democracy as the awaited Messiah. The conversation ends shortly after this, and the break is announced by the time: 'Un poco después de las siete...' (15). It can be seen therefore that although the conversation appears autonomous as a result of its separation through temporal phrases and 'en silencio', it is intimately tied to the rest of the narrative by individual words and allusions to the major themes and character traits.

Two general types of dialogue are identified by Rolfe (*31*, pp.343-46). One uses oblique references or silences (i.e. incomplete dialogue) to show political and social atmosphere, or to hide emotion. An example of political reference is: 'Siempre se me olvida que estamos en estado de sitio' (10). The example she gives of lack of emotion is that, after 'Nosotros somos huérfanos de nuestro hijo —dijo la mujer', no comment is made, thus increasing the poignancy (13; *31*, p.345). The second type is combative, ending in a jokey or stoic reply from the Colonel. This, Rolfe says, underlines the interior plot of the novel in that it shows the continuous battle against the Colonel's defences and how he retaliates. He resorts to humour, until the last dialogue, ending in 'mierda', when there is no recourse to jokes or stoicism. Rolfe restricts this type to the Colonel in response to his wife, but as the exchanges when the Colonel and his wife discuss the sale of the cock show, both have humour, but for different ends (54-56). The Colonel injects humour into what the old woman regards as a serious discussion: 'Así la vida es un soplo'; 'Eres idéntica al hombrecito de la avena Quaker'; but his wife also has some final words to say: 'Entonces está resuelto el problema. Ya se podrá contar con esa plata dentro de cincuenta años'; 'La cara del santo hace el milagro'. To maintain his resistance and defuse the situation, the Colonel uses a cliché and a joke, while his wife uses a cliché and an ironic remark about the problem being solved to show that bitterness and practicality mark her side of the inner conflict.

The Colonel's failure to tell her of his decision to sell the cock is a highly-charged silence: if he tells her, he will be showing her that he is giving in, renouncing his principles (55). She does not expect this of him, as she says when he expresses his sympathy for the employee dealing with his pension: 'Mal síntoma...Eso quiere decir que ya empiezas a resignarte' (46; again she has the last word). By his not telling her, their bickering continues. Saying that the Colonel has foreseen Sabas's replies (which we do not hear for a while) creates tension. In fact, Don Sabas upsets the Colonel's expectations by offering less than he had first said the cock was worth.

Rolfe's view of the the Colonel's humour is that it is an escape valve for him in his altercations with his wife. It is often directed at himself ('—Estás en el hueso pelado —dijo... Ya estoy encargado por una fábrica de clarinetes', 36), and it gets blacker as his situation worsens, so that it is tragicomic. But, she continues, like all the systems that García Márquez constructs in the novel (the Colonel's faith in illusions, the avoidance of emotions), the recourse to humour is broken by the last paragraph, when no illusions remain (*31*, p.343).

Vargas Llosa studies in detail the use of humour as a defuser, juxtaposing comic phrases (usually taken from a common oral fund) with bitter reality (*33*, pp.331-43). The Colonel's religious jokes (for instance those on p.23) compare with his wife's reliance on prayer, and her religious cliché (56). His jokes dissolve potentially overwhelming situations, as in: 'Esto empieza a parecerse al cuento del gallo capón' (28). Clichés are a rich source of humour in the novel. When used by someone other than the Colonel (like 'La cara del santo hace el milagro', 56, or 'Lo único que llega con seguridad es la muerte', 46), they provide a subtle balance, says Vargas Llosa, between the drama concentrated on the main protagonist and the character who observes or accompanies him (*33*, p.341). Nevertheless, clichés are an oral form of humour belonging to everyone; the Colonel uses them in order to laugh at himself: 'A buena hambre no hay mal pan' (36); 'El que espera lo mucho espera lo poco' (32). Of the second example, Rowe says that it is a 'vague and fatuous' statement which the Colonel uses literally. But the effect is not to make huge bureaucracy appear normal, rather a refusal to accept things as they are. Opposition is the natural response, seen here in the Colonel's desire to change lawyers after so much time. The accuracy of the humour eradicates the danger of the Colonel seeming naive (*32*). This extra dimension in the humour (its ability to rejuvenate clichés, to endow them with new meanings) is based to a large extent on irony. Therefore a cliché like 'A buena hambre no hay mal pan' is more significant than being part of what Pontiero calls 'a simple philosophy' (*1*, p.xxxix); it has a dual function: for the Colonel it is a form of comic relief, but for the reader, the irony uncovers the basis of suffering behind it. An example given by Ariza González is:

—Compras una libra de maíz —dijo la mujer—. Compras con los vueltos el café de mañana y cuatro onzas de queso.
—Y un elefante dorado para colgarlo en la puerta —prosiguió el coronel—. Sólo el maíz cuesta cuarenta y dos. (21)

Here the laughter is lost in sadness (*7*, p.21). While García Márquez injects humour into the narrative,[28] it has a special purpose, as Vargas Llosa says:

El humor en *El coronel no tiene quien le escriba* es pretexto para dotar de persuasión a los materiales de mayor patetismo y desmesura, o subterfugio para expresar —mediante una operación casi mágica en la que el humor deja de ser humor— una visión de la realidad que no es risueña en ningún sentido. (*33*, p.343)

While for the characters, humour defuses the drama, the irony prevents the neutralization of the situation (*30*, p.23). The conversations in the lawyer's office and at Don Sabas's house are particularly laden with irony. In the former, 'El que espera

[28] Humour is often lacking in Latin American writers, say Eyzaguirre, *17*, p.345, and Roger M. Peel, in 'The Short Stories of Gabriel García Márquez', *Studies in Short Fiction*, 8 (1971), 159-68, at p.166.

lo mucho espera lo poco' has already been discussed; another instance in this scene is:

> Se llenó los pulmones de un aire abrasante y pronunció la sentencia como si acabara de inventarla:
> —La unión hace la fuerza. (28)

It is obvious that the strength of unity has been useless as far as the Colonel is concerned; he says as much to the lawyer, and feels solitude for the first time. But the phrase has a deeper meaning: Colombia is riven by civil war, hinted at by the text, so since the concept of strength through unity has been lost, the lawyer's inventing the phrase is not so extraordinary (unity in Colombia would be strength). During the Colonel's first visit to Don Sabas, the irony in 'Dichoso usted que puede comerse un estribo de cobre' (43) must be apparent to the Colonel as well as to the reader. He knows full well that he does not have an iron stomach.

On his later visit, the doctor jokes to the Colonel at Don Sabas's expense:

> —Habrá que fusilarlo —dijo el médico dirigiéndose al coronel—. La diabetes es demasiado lenta para acabar con los ricos.
> 'Ya usted ha hecho lo posible con sus malditas inyecciones de insulina', dijo don Sabas, y dio un salto sobre sus nalgas fláccidas. 'Pero yo soy un clavo duro de morder.' (56-57)

As Vargas Llosa points out, this humorous exchange moderates Don Sabas's suffering and hides the true battle between the doctor and his patient, which is a conflict between social and political groups. The doctor can say what he really thinks of Don Sabas through humour, but the reader realises what Don Sabas does not (*33*, p.341). Don Sabas's remark that he is a tough nail to bite could equally apply to the Colonel, but on spiritual grounds, not in the egocentric way in which the rich man refers to himself. This irony is compounded by that of the

Colonel and his wife referring to Don Sabas as 'mi compadre' when he is nothing of the sort.

The irony in *El coronel*, according to Rolfe, is not satirical, but tragic; what is said and how it is said is different from what the narrative implies (*31*, pp.349 and 340). The efforts that the inhabitants of 'este pueblo de mierda' have to make in order to survive hint at a cruel political environment. It is not scorned or ridiculed by their words, pastimes or illusions, but condemns itself by inference. The tragedy lies in the fact that, in this atmosphere, the Colonel's thoughts and actions are portrayed as unique. His hopes and illusions, to which he clings resolutely in front of his wife and at the risk of appearing naïve to others, turn out to be an illusory strength when he realises that all that remains is excrement. In trying to survive by avoiding reality, he ends with a will to survive that accepts and confronts reality.

Irony is also to be found in the way in which the characters' words often reveal more about themselves or their situation than they intend. For example:

El coronel se sintió contagiado de un humor sombrío.
—Qué te pasa.
—Nada —dijo le mujer.
Él tuvo la impresión de que esta vez le había correspondido a ella el turno de mentir. (47)

By supposing that his wife is lying this time, the Colonel is not only admitting that she is subject to the humiliation imposed by their misery, but also that he too has to lie. As he says later: 'Lo peor de la mala situación es que lo obliga a uno a decir mentiras' (49). What the Colonel does not say is that while he may lie outside his house, he does not expect falsehoods between himself and his wife at home. But when the truth does come out it rarely helps:

—Estaba donde el padre Ángel —dijo—. Fui a solicitarle un préstamo sobre los anillos de matrimonio.
—¿Y qué te dijo?
—Que es pecado negociar con las cosas sagradas...

—Tampoco quieren el cuadro —dijo ella—. Casi todo el mundo tiene el mismo. Estuve donde los turcos.

El coronel se encontró amargo.

—De manera que ahora todo el mundo sabe que nos estamos muriendo de hambre. (49)

He uncovers her lie only to find that she has made obvious what he tries to hide by lying.

Earlier, his wife says, 'Siempre es mejor entenderse directamente' (34), a statement which can be interpreted as: she knows where she stands and is prepared to speak her mind. In relation to her husband it is ironic because he seldom makes his thoughts or intentions clear, even though he reaffirms his principles. It is also ironic if applied to their marital relationship because, at the end, there is little understanding between them. In terms of politics, one cannot make oneself understood for fear of being killed for opposing authority. In terms of the text itself, the style is direct, but there is much that is told by implication. García Márquez's appreciation of Hemingway and his knowledge of journalism are in evidence in this last respect. On the former he says:

> el consejo aquel de que un cuento, como el *iceberg*, debe estar sustentado en la parte que no se ve: en el estudio, la reflexión, el material reunido y no utilizado directamente en la historia. Sí, Hemingway le enseña a uno muchas cosas, inclusive a saber cómo un gato dobla una esquina. (*28*, p.43; see also *23*, p.324, *29*, p.60, *30*, p.18, and *33*, pp.41 and 150-56)

On journalism his opinion is:

> El lenguaje utilizado en *El coronel no tiene quien le escriba*, en *La mala hora* y en varios de los cuentos de *Los funerales de la Mamá Grande* es conciso, sobrio, dominado por una preocupación de eficacia, tomada del periodismo. (*28*, p.86)

He adds elsewhere: 'no aprendí el lenguaje económico y directo' from journalism, 'sino ciertos recursos legítimos para que los lectores crean la historia'.[29]

The techniques of impersonal narration (irony, changing points of view through juxtapositions, omissions and fragmented prose through cinematographic cutting, the creation of tension) paint a harsh picture of a closed environment in which the rich and poor alike suffer. These distancing techniques also prevent the reader from identifying completely or continually with any character, although their humour inspires sympathy (especially for the Colonel). When talking of García Márquez's short stories, Peel says that the author's affection for his characters shows that he is not an angry writer; he is critical, but does not indict Colombian society.[30] In *El coronel* the criticism of Colombia is seen in global terms:

> Hizo un esfuerzo para reaccionar contra su estómago. 'Desde que hay censura los periódicos no hablan sino de Europa', dijo. 'Lo mejor será que los europeos se vengan para acá y que nosotros nos vayamos para Europa. Así sabrá todo el mundo lo que pasa en su respectivo país.'
> —Para los europeos América del Sur es un hombre de bigotes, con una guitarra y un revólver —dijo el médico, riendo sobre el periódico—. No entienden el problema. (25)

That Europeans cannot comprehend the true nature of Latin America is a recurring topic (identified by Alejo Carpentier):[31]

> La palabra tempestad sugiere una cosa al lector europeo y

[29] Quoted in *16*, p.33. In this same volume, Mario Benedetti remarks on the reader's having to use imagination to draw conclusions: 'García Márquez o la vigilia del sueño', *16*, pp.99-105, at p.102; see also *10*, p.59. On reportage in García Márquez, see *8*, pp.51-53.

[30] Roger M. Peel, 'The Short Stories of Gabriel García Márquez', p.164. This view is not shared by Janes, who says that 'the effect of García Márquez's method is often brutal as the sentence simultaneously pins down the wriggling object of its contemplation and dismisses it, moving on and away' (*24*, p.112).

[31] See 'De lo real maravilloso americano', particularly pp.115-21.

otra a nosotros, y lo mismo ocurre con la palabra lluvia,que nada tiene que ver con los diluvios torrenciales del trópico.(*28*, p.85)

In the case of *El coronel*, it is not just natural phenomena that a foreigner might not understand; the implication is that the political situation would be so brutally alien to European eyes, that to report it in any other way than by implication would cause incredulity.

Pontiero repeats García Márquez's intention 'that the good novelist will convince even the censors, not by persuading them that they are wrong but by offering them a novel that is aesthetically irresistible' (*1*, p.xliii). In García Márquez's own opinion, 'En realidad, el deber de un escritor, y el deber revolucionario, si se quiere, es el de escribir bien' (*28*, pp.83-84). As Wayne C. Booth says:

in fiction the concept of writing well must include the successful ordering of your reader's view of a fictional world. The 'well-made phrase' in fiction must be much more than 'beautiful'; it must serve larger ends, and the artist has a moral obligation, contained as an essential part of his aesthetic obligation to 'write well', to do all that is possible in any given instance to realize his world as he intends it.[32]

There can be little doubt that in *El coronel no tiene quien le escriba*, García Márquez has selected elements from his world so carefully, and portrayed them so precisely, that even a European reader has no qualms about siding with a veteran who, after fifty-six years, still awaits his pension with firm resolve and a sense of humour.

---

[32] *The Rhetoric of Fiction* (Chicago: University of Chicago Press, 1961), p.388.

Bibliographical Note

The most thorough bibliographies of the life and work of Gabriel García Márquez are: Margaret Eustella Fau, *García Márquez: An Annotated Bibliography, 1947-79* (Westport, Con.: Greenwood Press, 1980), and Margaret Eustella Fau and Nelly Sfeir de Gonzalez, compilers, *Bibliographic Guide to Gabriel García Márquez, 1979-1985* (New York, Westport, London: Greenwood Press, 1986).

A. EDITIONS OF 'EL CORONEL NO TIENE QUIEN LE ESCRIBA'

1. Edited with Introduction, Notes and Vocabulary by Giovanni Pontiero (Manchester: University Press, 1981). Has a 43-page introduction, with chronology, select bibliography, notes, and vocabulary. There are several other editions. Two annotated editions are *El coronel* with *La increíble y triste historia de la cándida Eréndira y de su abuela desalmada*. Selección y estudio preliminar por Noé Jitrik (Buenos Aires: Librería del Colegio, 1976), and that in the Colección Austral, with an introduction by Joaquín Marco (Madrid: Espasa-Calpe, 1986). Four unannotated editions are: Mexico City: Biblioteca Era, 1963; Buenos Aires: Editorial Sudamericana, 1968; Barcelona: Plaza y Janés, 1974; and Madrid: Mondadori España, 1987. An English translation is available: *No One Writes to the Colonel*, translated by J.S. Bernstein, in a volume with *Big Mama's Funeral* (London: Picador-Pan Books, 1979).

B. SELECTED OTHER WORKS BY GARCÍA MÁRQUEZ

2. *Todos los cuentos de Gabriel García Márquez (1947-1972)* (Barcelona: Plaza y Janés, 1975). Contains the collections: *Ojos de perro azul, Los funerales de la Mamá Grande*, and *La increíble y triste historia de la cándida Eréndira y de su abuela desalmada*.
3. *La hojarasca* (Buenos Aires: Editorial Sudamericana, 1972).
4. *La mala hora* (Buenos Aires: Editorial Sudamericana, 1974).
5. *Cien años de soledad* (Buenos Aires: Editorial Sudamericana, 1967).
6. *Crónica de una muerte anunciada* (Barcelona: Editorial Bruguera, 1981).

Subsequent to the preparation of this guide, García Márquez has published two further major novels, *El amor en los tiempos del cólera* (Barcelona: Bruguera, 1985) and *El general en su laberinto* (Madrid: Mondadori, 1989) as well as several shorter works.

C. CRITICISM

There are a number of collections of essays on García Márquez which are
useful either as background or as material for studies of specific texts.
Essays relevant to *El coronel* are given below. Among the collections are:
Books Abroad, 47, no.3 (1973), 439-505; *Gabriel García Márquez*, edited
by Peter G. Earle, Persiles, 129 (Madrid: Taurus, 1981); *Homenaje a
Gabriel García Márquez: variaciones interpretativas en torno a su obra*,
edited by Helmy F. Giacoman (New York: Las Americas, 1972); *Magazine
Littéraire*, no.178 (1981), 14-35; *Nueve asedios a García Márquez* (Santiago
de Chile: Editorial Universitaria, 1969); 'Supplement on Gabriel García
Márquez *One Hundred Years of Solitude'*, *70 Review*, edited by Ronald
Christ (New York: Center for Inter-American Relations, 1971), 97-191;
Sobre García Márquez, compiled by Pedro Simón Martínez, Colección Puño
y Letra, 1 (Montevideo: Biblioteca de la Marcha, 1971; first published
Havana: Casa de las Américas, 1969), *Critical Perspectives on Gabriel
García Márquez*, edited by Bradley A. Shaw and Nora Vera-Godwin
(Lincoln, Nebraska: Society of Spanish and Spanish-American Studies,
1986); *En el punto de mira: Gabriel García Márquez*, edited by Ana María
Hernández de López (Madrid: Pliegos, 1985); *Gabriel García Márquez and
the Powers of Fiction*, edited by Julio Ortega with the assistance of Claudia
Elliott (Austin: University of Texas Press, 1988).

7. Ariza González, Julio, 'La espera: constante universal del hombre: *El
    coronel no tiene quien le escriba*', *Sin Nombre*, 4, no.3 (1974), 13-29.
    The theme of waiting and its effect on the character of the Colonel.

8. Arnau, Carment, *El mundo mítico de Gabriel García Márquez*, Nueva
    Colección Ibérica, 36 (Barcelona: Ediciones Península, 1971). Looks
    for constants in García Márquez's work up to *Cien años de soledad*; *El
    coronel* and *La mala hora* are said to fall outside the overall scheme of
    the works.

9. Blanco Aguinaga, Carlos, 'Sobre la lluvia y la historia en las ficciones
    de García Márquez', in *Narradores hispanoamericanos de hoy*, edited
    by Juan Bautista Avalle-Arce, University of North Carolina Studies in
    the Romance Languages and Literatures: Symposia, 1 (Chapel Hill,
    1973), pp.55-71. Stimulating study of rain and its symbolic relationship
    with history up to *Cien años*; does not concentrate on any one novel or
    story.

10. Bollettino, Vincenzo, *Breve estudio de la novelística de García
    Márquez* (Madrid: Playor, 1973), pp.47-64, *'El coronel no tiene quien
    le escriba'*. Discusses the techniques of impersonal narration employed
    in the novel.

11. Castagnino, Raúl H., *'Sentido' y estructura narrativa* (Buenos Aires:
    Editorial Nova, 1975). An application of the principles of structuralist
    analysis to *El coronel*.

12. Conte, Rafael, *lenguaje y violencia. Introducción a la nueva novela hispanoamericana.* (Madrid: Al-Borak, 1972), pp.157-83, 'Gabriel García Márquez o el mito'. Résumé of García Márquez's life, work and influences.

13. Dario Carrillo, Germán, *La narrativa de Gabriel García Márquez (Ensayos de interpretación)* (Madrid: Ediciones de Arte y Bibliofilia, 1975). Nothing definite on *El coronel*, but wide-ranging study of narrative techniques; includes an interview, and a discussion of *33*.

14. Dauster, Frank, 'The Short Stories of García Márquez', *Books Abroad*, 47 (1973), 466-70. Good background on the short stories, but not specifically on *El coronel*.

15. Dorfman, Ariel, 'La muerte como acto imaginativo en *Cien años de soledad*', in *Homenaje a Gabriel García Márquez*, pp.105-40. Although principally about *Cien años*, deals also with the conflict between man and his environment in the other works, including *El coronel*.

16. Durán, Armando, 'Conversaciones con Gabriel García Márquez', in *Sobre García Márquez*, pp.31-41 (translated into English in *70 Review*, 109-19). García Márquez's own opinions on influences on his writing, and on his political attitudes to writing.

17. Eyzaguirre, Luis B., *El héroe en la novela hispanoamericana del siglo XX* (Santiago de Chile: Editorial Universitaria, 1973), pp.323-46, 'Gabriel García Márquez: la conquista del tiempo'. Contains a concise résumé and study of the major themes and characters of *El coronel*.

18. Fernández-Braso, Miguel, *Gabriel García Márquez: una conversación infinita* (Madrid: Editorial Azur, 1969). An extensive interview covering García Márquez's life and work and his attitudes to writing and politics.

19. Franco, Jean, 'El mundo grotesco de García Márquez', *Índice*, no.237 (November, 1968), 37. Myth in the work of García Márquez, characterized, according to convention, by exaggeration and the grotesque.

20. Gilard, Jacques, 'Un immense discours sur la mort', *Magazine Littéraire*, 15-19. A thorough study of the early stoies and novels, including *El coronel*.

21. González Bermejo, Ernesto, *Cosas de escritores* (Montevideo: Biblioteca de Marcha, 1971), pp.11-51, 'Con Gabriel García Márquez: ahora doscientos años de soledad'. An interview, shorter than, but as useful as, *18*; contains a little more information on *El coronel*.

22. Gullón Ricardo, 'García Márquez o el ovidado arte de contar', in *Homenaje a Gabriel García Márquez*, pp.143-70. Mainly on *Cien años*, but contains much useful material on general aspects of García Márquez's style.

23. Harss, Luis, and Barbara Dohmann, *Into the Mainstream. Conversations with Latin American Writers* (New York: Harper and

Row, 1967 — originally published as *Los nuestros*, Buenos Aires: Editorial Sudamericana, 1966), pp.310-41, 'Gabriel García Márquez, or the Lost Chord'. *El coronel* discussed, mainly in terms of character and style, together with work before *Cien años*.

24. Janes, Regina, *Gabriel García Márquez:Revolutions in Wonderland* A Literary Frontiers Edition (Columbia: University of Missouri Press, 1981). A general study of García Márquez's writings and politics up to 1979.

25. McMurray, George R., *Gabriel García Márquez* (New York: Frederick Ungar Publishing Co., 1977). A good general study; *El coronel* is discussed on pp.21-32 in a chapter with *La mala hora* on *La Violencia*.

26. Maturo, Graciela, *Claves simbólicas de Gabriel García Márquez* (Buenos Aires: Fernando García Cambeiro, 1972), pp.105-14, 'Tiempo mítico y salvación en *El coronel no tiene quien le escriba*'. Questionable conclusion that, although García Márquez is not taking a religious stance, all his symbols are drawn from a Western Christian tradition.

27. Mejía Duque, Jaime, 'Mito y realidad en Gabriel García Márquez', in René Jara and Jaime Mejía, *Las claves del mito en Gabriel García Márquez* (Valparaíso: Ediciones Universitarias de Valparaíso, 1972), pp.57-93. On García Márquez as a representative of Latin American fiction writing; his style and use of myth.

28. Mendoza, Plinio Apuleyo, and Gabriel García Márquez, *El olor de la guayaba* (Barcelona: Editorial Bruguera, 1982). Conversations covering the same ground as *16,18,21*, but encompassing, in addition, García Márquez's most recent writing and political activities.

29. Rama, Angel, 'Un novelista de la violencia americana', in *Homenaje a Gabriel García Márquez*, pp.57-72. On *El coronel* and *La mala hora* in which violence is equated with political oppression; García Márquez's expression of violence.

30. Rodríguez Monegal, Emir, 'Novedad y anacronismo de *Cien años de soledad*', in *Homenaje a Gabriel García Márquez*, pp.13-42. Thematic and narrative anachronism; although concerned with *Cien años*, has a useful section on *El coronel* in relation to the other works.

31. Rolfe, Doris, 'El arte de la concentración expresiva en *El coronel no tiene quien le escriba*', *Cuadernos Hispanoamericanos*, nos 277-78 (1973), 337-50. Thorough study of the style of *El coronel*, in which traditional techniques are said to be used unconventionally, giving the novel individuality.

32. Rowe, William, 'Gabriel García Márquez', BBC Series *Study on 4, Twentieth-Century Spanish Authors*, first broadcast 25 May, 1982; unpublished, but brief Study Notes entitled *Modern Spanish Writers* are available from the BBC on request. Excellent short talk on García Márquez's writing, devoting much time to *El coronel*.

33. Vargas Llosa, Mario, *García Márquez: historia de un deicidio*
(Barcelona: Barral Editores; Caracas: Monte Avila Editores, 1971). An
exhaustive study of García Márquez's life and work. Pp.293-343 deal
exclusively with *El coronel*: ' "El pueblo": el idealismo optimista'.

34. ———, 'García Márquez: de Aracataca a Macondo', in *La novela
hispanoamericana actual*, compiled by Angel Flores and Raúl Silva
Cáceres (New York: Las Americas, 1971), pp.157-75; also in *Nueve
asedios a García Márquez*, pp.126-46, and translated into English, in
70 Review, pp.129-43. Biography and literary history, abbreviated from
33.

35. Volkening, Ernesto, 'Anotado al margen de *Cien años de soledad*', in
Nueva novela latinoamericana, Vol.I, compiled by Jorge Lafforgue
(Buenos Aires: Editorial Paidós, 1969), pp.142-79. The relationship
between *Cien años* and other works previous to it, in terms of
character, style and motives.

36. ———, 'Gabriel García Márquez o el trópico desembrujado', in
Homenaje a Gabriel García Márquez, pp.73-86. Good article on the
emphasis on weather and the tropical setting of García Márquez's work,
leading to a discussion of related themes and images.

37. Woods, Richard D., 'Time and Futility in the Novel *El coronel no tiene
quien le escriba*', *Kentucky Romance Quarterly*, 17 (1970), 287-95.
Time is seen as the basis on which the theme of futility is expressed in
the novel.

The body of critical work on García Márquez has grown significantly since
the first publication of this guide in 1984. In addition to the collections of
essays, post-1984, mentioned above, it is worth mentioning here: Raymond
L. Williams, *Gabriel García Márquez*, Twayne World Authors Series 749
(Boston: Twayne, 1984), pp.57-60 deal specifically with *El coronel*; Stephen
Minta, *Gabriel García Márquez: Writer of Colombia* (London: Cape, 1987),
chapter 3, "Two Stories of the Violencia", pp.65-92, discusses *El coronel*
and *La mala hora*; María Victoria Giralda Pérez, Esperanza Ortega
Martínez, María Socorro Pérez González, *El coronel no tiene quien le
escriba de Gabriel García Márquez*, Guía de lectura 3 (Madrid: Akal, 1987).

D. HISTORICAL BACKGROUND

38. Bergquist, Charles W., *Coffee and Conflict in Colombia, 1886-1910*
(Durham, N.C.: Duke University Press, 1978).

39. Galbraith, W.O., *Colombia: A General Survey* (London: Oxford
University Press, for the Royal Institute of International Affairs, 1953;
2nd edition, 1966).

40. Guzmán Campos, Germán, *La violencia en Colombia: parte
descriptiva* (Cali: Ediciones Progreso, 1968).

41. Martz, John D., *Colombia: a Contemporary Political Survey* (Chapel Hill: University of North Carolina Press, 1962).
42. Tamayo, Joaquín, *La revolución de 1899*, Biblioteca Banco Popular, 76 (Bogotá, 1975).

CRITICAL GUIDES TO SPANISH TEXTS

Edited by
J.E. Varey and A.D. Deyermond